*Oxford
Secondary
English*

Dimensions

Book 4

John Seely
Frank Green
Graham Nutbrown

Oxford University Press   1989

Contents

Section A

Section B: stories and poems

Oxford University Press, Walton Street, Oxford OX2 6DP

Oxford New York Toronto
Delhi Bombay Calcutta Madras Karachi
Petaling Jaya Singapore Hong Kong Tokyo
Nairobi Dar es Salaam Cape Town
Melbourne Auckland

and associated companies in
Berlin Ibadan

Oxford is a trade mark of Oxford University Press

© Oxford University Press 1989
First published 1989

ISBN 0 19 833171 1

Typeset by Best-set Typesetter Ltd, Hong Kong
Printed in Singapore

You have probably read or heard about strange, unidentified creatures being sighted in different parts of the world. Some people believe they exist, others believe they are just legends. (In the United Kingdom, the Loch Ness Monster is the most famous.)

This unit is about the evidence for strange creatures that resemble human beings. The best known is the Yeti or Abominable Snowman, but the region with the most sightings is North America where such creatures are called Bigfoot.

English activities

This unit gives you practice in the following:

- group discussion
- assessing written evidence
- assessing pictorial evidence
- judging written arguments and opinions
- expressing and justifying your own opinions
- tabulating information
- making notes
- writing: a report, an article, a story

Portrait of Bigfoot

Different reports mention different aspects of Bigfoot.

Smell

'like unwashed armpits'
'it stank like a half-rotten bear hide'
'like a dog that hasn't been bathed in a year and suddenly gets rained on'

Noises

Rich Knovich was staying in his cabin in Scotch Run Valley, Pennsylvania, USA, in 1980, when he and his relatives were woken by a loud, high-pitched crying sound which was not recognisable.

'It was one heck of a weird yell.'

Outside the dogs were cowering in their pens.

Shots

Charles Fulton of Kentucky shot at a white-haired Bigfoot in October 1980. Two shots with a .22 calibre pistol had no effect.

Mr Sites, a farmer in New Jersey, USA, fired at a Bigfoot which kept coming to his farm in May 1977. He used a .410 shot-gun and fired three or four shots.

'The Bigfoot simply growled at me.'

Disappearance

In Uniontown, Pennsylvania, in 1974, a woman shot at a tall, hairy, ape-like creature at her front door, using a shot-gun kept by the door to frighten dogs away. As the creature raised its arms above its head, the woman pointed the gun and fired. The creature disappeared in a flash of light.

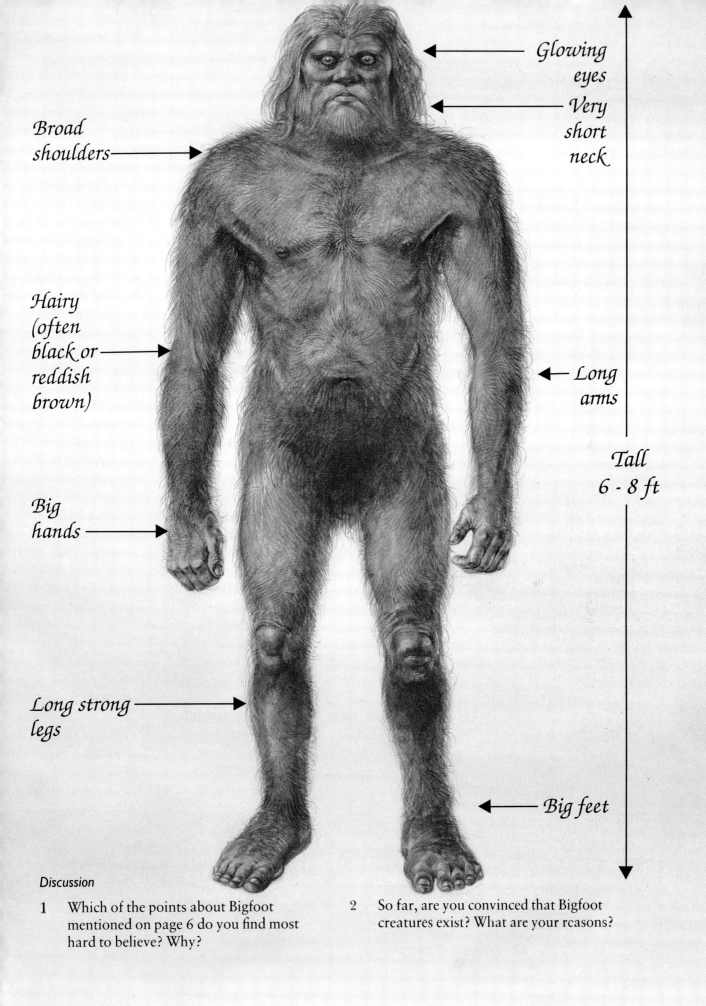

Glowing eyes

Very short neck

Broad shoulders

Hairy (often black or reddish brown)

Long arms

Big hands

Tall 6 - 8 ft

Long strong legs

Big feet

Discussion

1   Which of the points about Bigfoot mentioned on page 6 do you find most hard to believe? Why?

2   So far, are you convinced that Bigfoot creatures exist? What are your reasons?

Eye-witness reports

Many reports of Bigfoot sightings have to be ignored by the experts because the reports are unreliable. Some are obviously hoaxes or tricks. A **reliable** report may not turn out to be a true one but at least it will be worth investigating further.

What to do

1   Study the **reliability chart** and think about **what** each point means and **why** it is important.
    For each point make notes on:
    a)   why you think it is important.
    b)   examples of details which might make a report **more** or **less** reliable.

> Point 1: witness
> a) Some witnesses unreliable.
> Better to have more than 1.
> b) Report more reliable:
>   if by experienced person,
>   eg hunter, forest ranger.
>   less reliable
>   if witness young,
>   if vision poor

2   On the opposite page is an eye-witness report. Imagine that you are an expert investigator. You have been called in to examine it.
    a)   Read it carefully.
    b)   Copy out the reliability chart.
    c)   Fill it in for Donald Hepworth's report. (Use the notes you made to help you.)

Point	Details
1. WITNESS(ES): Who saw the beast?	
2. LOCATION Exactly where was it, when seen?	
3. DISTANCE How far away from the witness(es)?	
4. TIME Date/hour of the sighting?	
5. DURATION For how many minutes was the beast seen?	
6. CONDITIONS Weather and light at the time?	
7. DESCRIPTION Details to be provided.	
RELIABILITY REPORT: Would you recommend further investigation? (Please give your reasons.)	

Signed...

Donald Hepworth

Witness: Donald Hepworth, aged 54. He was working as Chief Inspector with the Ontario Humane Society, which involved working with bears and apes. He had previously worked with Canadian Military Intelligence and with the London Metropolitan Police. In the early evening of 7th April 1980, he was driving alone along US Highway 95 through Payette National Park in Idaho when he saw two Bigfoots. It was getting dark but the creatures were illuminated by his car headlamps.

I was flabbergasted! At a distance of perhaps 8 to 10 yards (7-9 metres), I could see their bodies were covered in hair that was short and black as a Labrador Retriever's. One was walking a few steps ahead of the other and appeared to be clutching something to its left upper torso (body). The one behind was an inch or two taller than the first; I would guess it to be five foot seven or eight inches (1.7 metres) in height as measured against the windscreen of the car. This creature half-turned towards me, and for a moment, I could see the flash of a white eyeball .... I noticed too its hands - thick, elongated and strong-looking.

Their heads were low-set on broad shoulders and their skulls were flat and sloped back from heavy brow ridges to a sort of conical topknot ... Their bodies were gangly rather than heavy or muscular, and perhaps because of this I had the distinct impression that they were young or youthful members of their species. I cannot remember detecting facial features, nor can I say whether this part of their anatomy was dark skin or dark hair ...

To the right of my car there was a sharp vertical six foot (1.8 metre) high embankment that on the other side dropped away quite steeply. The smaller creature paused at the foot of this incline, then flexing its legs in a standing broad jump posture, sprang easily to the top. It then dropped over the other side from my view. The larger creature quickly followed, ascending the bank in two steps, as effortlessly as a man might go upstairs. It was an extraordinary display of locomotion (movement); impossible, I am convinced, for any human to duplicate (copy).

Evidence

Eye-witness reports are all very well but even when they seem to be reliable they cannot replace hard evidence that can be examined by scientists.

Examples of the kind of evidence that has been found are:

    footprints
    faeces, or excreta
    hair samples.

Scientists who have studied samples of these do not agree amongst themselves whether they really prove that man-beasts exist. Unfortunately the best evidence – a man-beast creature itself, either dead or alive – has not been found.

Photographs

You might think that a photograph would be excellent evidence, but it is often not as reliable as it seems. The most impressive photograph of a man-beast was taken by Roger Patterson at Bluff Creek in California in 1967. He took a few seconds of movie film as the Bigfoot moved away from him, from a distance of 80 feet (24 metres). If this film is a hoax, it is a brilliant one. So, is this what a Bigfoot really looks like?

What to do

Discussion

1   Can you think of any reasons for distrusting photographs?
2   How does the creature Patterson filmed compare with the creatures you have read about in this unit so far?
3   Some people say they can see a baby clinging to the creature in Patterson's film. What do you think?

Writing

1   Copy and complete the reliability chart for this sighting.
2   Make a list of questions that you would like to put to Roger Patterson.
3   Write a paragraph expressing your opinion of the reliability of this evidence.

What's your opinion?

"I'd like to believe in bigfoots and I admit they look like some relative of prehistoric man but I just can't see how they could have survived separately from humans for so long. Where are their dens or hideouts? Why hasn't a single one ever been captured or killed?"

"I think they do exist. I think they could be related to some kind of pre-historic humans."

"I don't think the reports are all hoaxes but I think what the people have seen are animals such as bears or apes."

"I agree with the people who say bigfoots do not exist. I think the reports are hoaxes and the evidence such as footprints and photographs are forgeries."

What to do

1 Think about each of these points of view in turn. Consider what you have learned from the eye-witness reports and the information about evidence such as footprints and photographs.
2 Make detailed notes on each possibility, both for and against that point of view.

Group discussion

In a group of three or four discuss the evidence for Bigfoots and prepare to report back to the rest of the class what your group thinks.

1 Use the notes you have made.
2 Try to reach an agreed decision.
   If you can agree make notes summing up what you think and why.
   If you can't agree make notes summing up the main differences of opinion expressed.
3 Decide how you will report your findings back to the rest of the class.

Developments

1 Inventing an eye-witness report

You have to make up your own eye-witness report of a Bigfoot or some other monster. (You can set it in any part of the world.)

Here are some ideas to help you:

a) Decide whether you want to make this a reliable report or an unreliable report.

b) Look at the seven points which affect the reliability of a report (on page 8) and work out details for each one, to include in your report.

2 Encyclopaedia article

Write an article for a children's encyclopaedia about these creatures. Your article should be about 300 words long.

You should make sure that it includes:

a) details about what they look like
b) what parts of the world they have most often been sighted in
c) what evidence there is for their existence
d) some references to eye-witness reports
e) alternative explanations for what they might be.

You are writing this for 10 to 12-year-olds, so you have to make sure that you write in a fairly simple and clear style and that you explain things well.

3 Story for young children

Write a story for young children (between 5 and 7) about a baby Bigfoot or Yeti. Illustrate the story with your own pictures. Make sure that the story is not too scary or violent and make the language you use easy for young children to understand and enjoy.

a) Write the story in rough.
b) Ask someone to read it and suggest changes.
c) Write the story again, neatly, with only a few sentences on each page.
d) Draw the illustrations on separate pages.
e) Put the pages together.
f) Make a cover.
g) Try it out on a young child!

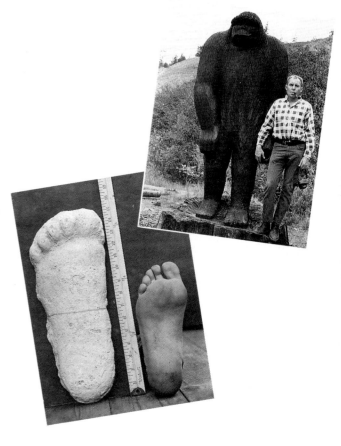

Coursework

You could include in your coursework folder not only the writing you do after reading this page, but also the notes and tables you have produced for the rest of the unit. These lead up to the assignments on this page and so are part of the **process** of producing the writing.

Self-assessment

Look at the list of **English activities** on page 5. Use it as a guide to remind you of what you have covered. Write a brief assessment of your work on this unit:

- what you did
- what you found easy or difficult
- what you found interesting or boring
- what you think you did well
- areas where you need more practice
- what you think you learned from the unit
- your overall impression of the work

Newsdesk

This unit is about the newsroom in a local radio station. You play the part of a member of the news team.

Organisation

There are four people in the team. Together you have to prepare and broadcast a seven-minute newscast.

Before you start give each person in the team a letter: A, B, C, D.

RADIO OURPLACE
News schedule

Item	Time available
National and international news	1 minute 30 secs to 2 minutes 00 secs
Local news	4 min. 30 secs to 5 min. 00 secs
Weather forecast & report on road conditions	30 secs.
Total time available	7.00 minutes

English activities

The unit contains these activities:

- working in groups:
  planning
  problem-solving and decision-making
  discussion
  presentation
- reading aloud
- reading and assessing news items
- role-play: interviews
- making notes
- writing a report

National and international news

Rail fares up 5%.

Child knocked down and killed on a charity walk.

Quads, born six weeks ago to kidney transplant patient,
go home.

The report of an official enquiry into the Midlands
Express train disaster blames computer malfunction.

Latest opinion poll delights opposition. Government
support down to 31%.

Customs officials begin work-to-rule. All-out strikes
threatened for holiday period.

In Northumberland, Norman, the 3-year-old border collie
trapped in a disused mineshaft for two days, has been
rescued.

British Aerospace announce advance orders worth £10
billion for their new DVI laser system, creating up to
1,000 new jobs.

Employment Minister, Sarah Colburn, faced tough
questions in the House of Commons following the
publication of the latest unemployment figures.

Three of the four men who escaped from police custody
in Birmingham yesterday have been recaptured. The fourth
man is said to be dangerous.

Car bomb explosion in Northern Spain kills three.

USSR to expel fourteen British diplomats in retaliation
for the fourteen Russian Embassy officials expelled
from Britain last week.

East-West peace talks now in doubt. US upset by
Russian criticism of American involvement in South and
Central America.

The condition of Pau-Pau, baby panda born at Peking
zoo two weeks ago is causing concern. Next 48 hours
crucial.

Spanish Tourist Board considering ban on holiday
bookings by groups of more than four male Britons.
This follows complaints from other foreign holiday-
makers in recent years.

The trial in Rome of 33 Mafia leaders, facing a total
of 874 charges, began amidst unprecedented security
cover. The trial, which is expected to last at least
8 months, will hear evidence from over 500 witnesses.

Nudist wedding ceremony in Florida, USA, held up
because best man could not produce the wedding ring.
He said he had nowhere to keep it.

Charles Dexter, 82, veteran Hollywood actor, born
Ourplace, UK, died at his home in Bel Air. Ill with
chest infection for 6 months.

What to do

1   Before you begin work as a group, each person should read *everything* on these two pages.

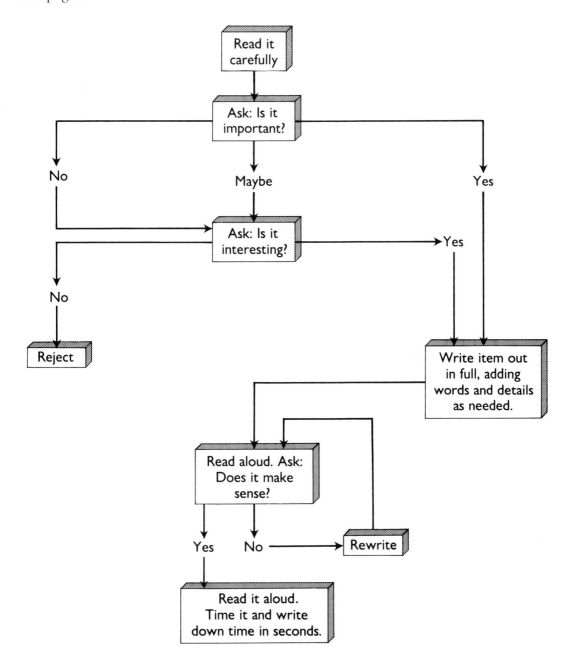

2   Now, as a group, follow this flow-chart for *each item*.

3   When you have done that for all the items, collect together the items you want to use.

4   Add up the times.

5   If they come to less than 90 seconds, you need to add material.

6   If they come to more than 120 seconds, you need to remove material.

7   When you have the right amount of material, decide on the best order for it.

Local events

This calendar of local events has been passed to you.

```
LOCAL EVENTS

6 p.m. today - 6 p.m. tomorrow

7.30 p.m.          Manor Street Youth Club.  Local residents to meet
                   leaders and members to discuss noise and unruly
                   behaviour.

8.30 p.m.          Town Hall.  Candidates in local by-election gather
                   for the count.  (Polling booths close 8.00 p.m.)
                   Election caused by death of Cllr. Mary Morgan, in
                   car accident.

9.00 p.m.          Black Horse Hotel.  Charity dinner and fashion
                   show in aid of World Wildlife Fund.  (Rumours of
                   'important' guest!).

10.00 p.m.         Town Hall.  Local by-election result expected.
- midnight

7.30 a.m.          Railway Station.  Arrival of MP, Mary Lonigan, to
                   discuss proposed closure of Whickby Mattress
                   factory.  Striking workers expected in force.

8.00 a.m.          Fareton.  Mothers of infant and junior school
                   children will demonstrate against heavy lorries
                   using village as short-cut to motorway, instead of
                   A 666.

9.00 a.m.          Whickby Mattress Factory, Whickby.  Mary Lonigan
                   and management meet.  Statement promised -
                   expected between 10.45 a.m. and noon.  Union
                   meeting outside gates.

10.00 a.m.         Town Hall.  Area final of National Hairdressing
- 4.00 p.m.        Competition.  Winner qualifies for national final
                   at Olympia next month.

10.30 a.m.         Magistrates Court.  First appearance of three
                   youths on charges of vandalism and intimidation at
                   Edgefield.

2.00 p.m.          St. George's Street.  Pop star, Dizzy Plum, to
                   open Hizzenhurz boutique.

4.00 p.m.          "The Larches" Old Peoples Home, Fareton.  Mayor
                   and MP to congratulate Mrs Hilda Townsend, 100
                   years old.

4.14 p.m.          Flixby School.  Final rehearsal for "Baldy", a
                   musical written by two members of staff.  Students
                   and staff in cast.  First public performance
                   tomorrow.

5.00 p.m.          Clevely Road Sports Centre.  24-hour sponsored 5-
                   a-side football ends.
```

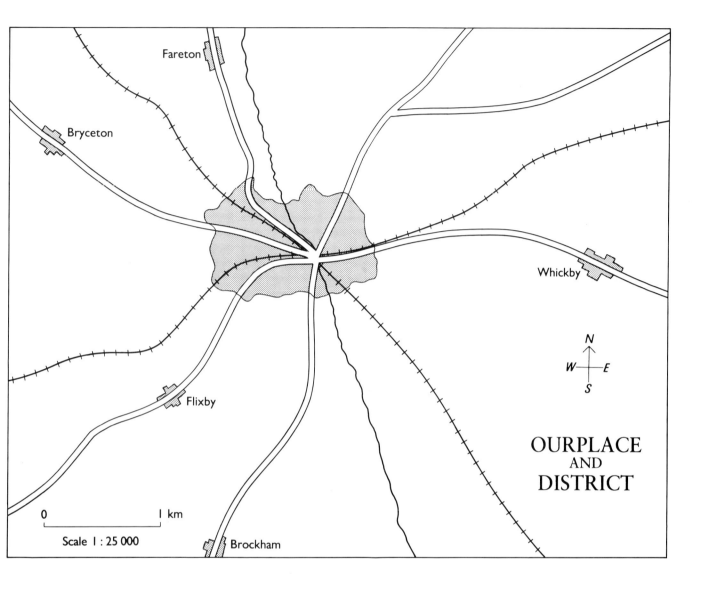

Fareton

Bryceton

Whickby

N
W—+—E
S

Flixby

0   1 km
Scale 1 : 25 000

OURPLACE
AND
DISTRICT

Brockham

What to do

1 Read the calendar carefully.
2 Decide which items will be of most interest and why.
3 Choose 4, 5 or 6 items you would like to cover.
4 For the next stage you will play these parts, based on the letters you gave yourselves at the start:
   A Reporter
   B Reporter
   C Assistant
   D Assistant
A and C will work together. B and D will work together.

5 Use the map and your list to work out which reporter can cover which stories. You may have to miss out some of the stories.
6 Write out your itinerary.

19

News assignment

Decide which of the news stories on pages 18 and 19 you are all going to work on. Each person in your group should have a letter, A, B, C, or D. Follow the instructions for your letter. (If there are five people in your group, the fifth person will have to 'share' a letter with one of the others.)

A

Working with C
1 Make a list of the people who would have information or ideas about the event.
2 Decide which one will be interviewed.

On your own
3 You are going to be the reporter. Decide what questions to ask.
4 Decide how you are going to record the answers.
5 Get everything ready.

Working with C
6 Interview C. Record the information and ideas you get from the interview.

Working as a group
7 Report back to the rest of the group, telling them what you learned from the interview.
8 Listen to what the others have to say.
9 Discuss how the story might be written up.
10 Write it up so that it lasts about a minute.
11 Discuss which other stories the group will report on. Divide them between the members of the group.
12 Write up your stories.

B

Working with D
1 Make a list of the people who would have information or ideas about the event.
2 Decide which one will be interviewed.

On your own
3 You are going to be the reporter. Decide what questions to ask.
4 Decide how you are going to record the answers.
5 Get everything ready.

Working with D
6 Interview D. Record the information and ideas you get from the interview.

Working as a group
7 Report back to the rest of the group, telling them what you learned from the interview.
8 Listen to what the others have to say.
9 Discuss how the story might be written up.
10 Write it up so that it lasts about a minute.
11 Discuss which other stories the group will report on. Divide them between the members of the group.
12 Write up your stories.

C

Working with A

1 Make a list of the people who would have information or ideas about the event.
2 Decide which one will be interviewed.

On your own

3 You are going to be that person. Think about who you are.
4 Make a note of: your name
your job
what kind of person you are.
5 Make a note of the main points of the news item: when it happened, who was involved and so on.
6 Decide how much of this you know, and *how* you know it.

Working with A

7 Now A will interview you about what happened and what you think about it.

Working as a group

8 Listen to what A and B have to say about their interviews.
9 Add any other information which you think should be included in the report.
10 Discuss how the story might be written up.
11 Write it up, as if you were a reporter. It should last about a minute.
12 Discuss which other stories the group will report on. Divide them between the members of the group.
13 Write up your stories.

D

Working with B

1 Make a list of the people who would have information or ideas about the event.
2 Decide which one will be interviewed.

On your own

3 You are going to be that person. Think about who you are.
4 Make a note of: your name
your job
what kind of person you are.
5 Make a note of the main points of the news item: when it happened, who was involved and so on.
6 Decide how much of this you know, and *how* you know it.

Working with B

7 Now B will interview you about what happened and what you think about it.

Working as a group

8 Listen to what A and B have to say about their interviews.
9 Add any other information which you think should be included in the report.
10 Discuss how the story might be written up.
11 Write it up, as if you were a reporter. It should last about a minute.
12 Discuss which other stories the group will report on. Divide them between the members of the group.
13 Write up your stories.

Exclusive!

On your way to another assignment something unexpected happens.

Working together

1 Decide what it is. You can choose one of the pictures or think of something different.

2 Think about the details. Between you, make a list of the main facts. Now you are going to have two interviews about what has happened.

3 Make a list of the best people to speak to.

Working alone

4 *Reporters* (A and B)
   a) Decide what questions to ask them.
   b) Decide how to record the answers.
   c) Get everything ready.

Assistants (C and D)
   a) Choose one of the people to be interviewed. You are going to be that person.
   b) Think about **who** you are and **what** you know and think. (As you did for the previous interview.)

Working in pairs (A + C, B + D)

5 When you are both ready, have the interview.

Working together

6 Now use the two interviews as the basis for a news report. Write it up so that it lasts between one and one and a half minutes.

Weather forecast

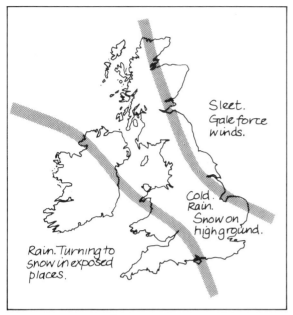

6 a.m. – noon

Noon – 6 p.m.

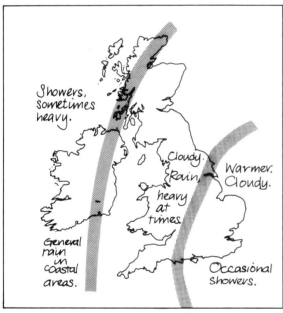

6 p.m. – midnight

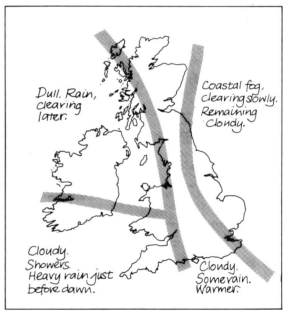

Midnight – 6 a.m.

What to do

Prepare the weather forecast for your own area for the twelve hours following your news bulletin:

1   Find the maps you need to use.
2   Find your area on the map.
3   Make notes on how the weather will change in the twelve hours after the news broadcast.
4   Use your notes as you write up the forecast.
5   If the weather will affect driving, finish the forecast with a report on road conditions.
6   Remember the time restriction on this part of the bulletin.

The broadcast

Now you are going to prepare the full news programme.

1 Begin by collecting all your material together.

Presentation

National and international news items will be read as short reports. **Local news items** can be presented in a number of ways:

- The newsreader gives the facts only.
- The newsreader introduces the reporter, who tells the story.
- The newsreader or the reporter tells the story and includes a recording of the interview.

2 Decide how each item should be presented.

Planning

You must follow the timings given on page 15.

3 Choose one newsreader for the whole broadcast or one for each of the three sections.
4 Make sure that all the other team members know what they are doing.
5 Have a practice run to see how long your material will take.
6 Decide how to alter the material so that it fits the time available.
7 Practise again until you have got the timings right.

Doing the broadcast

8 Now present your broadcast.

Working on this unit

A lot of the work in this unit can contribute to your spoken English assessment. The written reports you produced on pages 21 and 22 could be used in a folder of coursework.

Self-assessment

Look at the list of **English activities** on page 15. Use it as a guide to remind you of what you have covered. Write a brief assessment of your work on this unit:

- what you did
- what you found easy or difficult
- what you found interesting or boring
- what you think you did well
- areas where you need more practice
- what you think you learned from the unit
- your overall impression of the work

How much freedom?

TRIGWELL TIMES
6th March 1989

'SCHOOL A DISGRACE'
COMMENT BY COUNCIL CHAIRPERSON

In a meeting held last night Councillor Collins accused Mrs Freeman, The Head of Trigwell School, of being responsible for the undisciplined behaviour of the pupils.

He argued that the main problem with the pupils' behaviour was not one of attitude but of expecting more than was rightfully due to them.

He went on to say that the sort of behaviour he had witnessed was outrageous.

He talked exclusively to our reporter before the meeting and claimed that as a representative of the citizens of Trigwell he had every right to voice a generally-held view that the fault lay fairly and squarely at the door of the Head.

TRIGWELL TIMES
9th March 1989

HEAD FIGHTS BACK
CLAIMS UNJUST ACCUSATIONS

Mrs J.A. Freeman, in a letter to this newspaper, defended the school and explained the thinking behind her attitude to education.

She invited Councillor Collins to discuss directly with her any relevant issues.

This unit is about how schools should be organised and run. It is based on a school in an imaginary town called Trigwell. The unit is presented as a story and at each stage you are asked to comment on what happens and also, at times, to take part as one of the people involved.

English activities

In this unit you will undertake these activities:

- reading and understanding written arguments
- reading and understanding tabulated information
- judging and commenting on arguments
- reflecting and commenting on personal experience
- writing a newspaper report
- writing an extended argument
- role-play

'. . . and the townspeople find the behaviour of children at the school unacceptable. For a start they don't have to wear school uniform, and as a result some of them wear the most outlandish clothes. I saw two girls the other day going into the school wearing boilersuits! You can't have discipline in a school unless the pupils are made to wear a proper school uniform.

As far as I can see the school's policy is to let them do exactly as they please – they don't have to attend lessons if they don't feel like . . . **and** they don't have to explain to anyone why not. I ask you, how can you possibly expect children to learn anything in such a situation?

There's no discipline, no manners, no respect. They're even allowed to call the teachers by their first names. As a result the children think they can treat adults as equals. I spoke to a group of boys from the school the other day, and I was shocked by the way they replied. They disagreed with what I was saying, and even told me that I didn't have my facts right. One of them had the cheek to call me Maurice! Now in my day . . .'

SCHOOL 'A DISGRACE'
Comment by a Council Leader

At the Council meeting held last night, Councillor M. E. Collins accused Trigwell School of being responsible for the undisciplined behaviour of local children.

What to do

1   Make a list of the main things Councillor Collins thinks are wrong with the school.
2   For each one, say **why** he thinks that it is wrong.
3   For each one, say whether you think he gives good reasons or not.
4   Write five or six lines of what you think he went on to say.

TRIGWELL SCHOOL

Head Teacher: J. A. Freeman M.A. (Oxon)

September 15, 1987

The Editor
The Trigwell Times

Dear Sir,

In response to Councillor Collins' attack on members of this school, as reported in your newspaper, I feel I must put the record straight.

We see this school as a place where everyone is involved equally in education : teachers and pupils are partners sharing a common experience. It therefore seems silly for pupils to have to call their teachers "Sir" or "Miss", as though they were servants, or to be forced to wear a uniform as if they were soldiers or prisoners.

You can't force people to be educated. They've got to want to learn. So lessons must be voluntary. Pupils soon find out that missing a subject, or even a single lesson is boring and not in their own interests. We nearly always find that once they have got over the shock of their new "freedom", they settle down and attend lessons regularly and enthusiastically. However, Councillor Collins and his supporters will be relieved to know that any pupils who do miss lessons regularly are asked to come and discuss things with me. We usually manage to work things out sensibly.

...and I am very willing to discuss with Councillor Collins anything about the school which is still troubling him.

Yours faithfully,

What to do

1   The Head Teacher explains the reasons behind some of the things that Councillor Collins is complaining about. Make a list of his complaints. Against each one, sum up what Mrs Freeman says in reply.

2   For each of Mrs Freeman's explanations, write two or three sentences expressing your own opinions.

Miriam gives her views

Reporter: You're in the fourth form, aren't you?

Miriam: Yes, that's right.

Reporter: How come you don't have school uniform like kids at other schools?

Miriam: School uniform? Don't be silly. Why should anyone want to dress like everyone else?

Reporter: All the other schools do it.

Miriam: We don't think like them. We're all equal here and we're allowed to wear what we like. Wearing school uniform doesn't make you work any better.

Reporter: A lot of people think so.

Miriam: Uniform is just a way of keeping kids under control – like a flock of sheep.

Reporter: You've got to have discipline. Another thing I've heard is that you don't have any punishments – for people who won't do as they're told.

Miriam: You've got it all wrong. Telling people what to do isn't the way to get them interested in anything. School should be optional. Nobody should be forced to do things. You never learn anything like that.

Reporter: So what happens if somebody just doesn't go to lessons?

Miriam: Then they don't go, it's as simple as that. If they're forced to go to a lesson they don't like, they won't learn anything anyway. Our way we're all volunteers who **want** to learn.

Reporter: What happens if people misbehave in a lesson – fool about?

Miriam: They don't.

Reporter: But if they did?

Miriam: The others would soon tell them to shut up – they **want** to learn.

Reporter: Some people think school should be tough and competitive.

Miriam: That's rubbish – the tougher things are in school, the more the kids will rebel against education. People who think school should be tough are living in the past. Schools have got to change with the times.

Reporter: And you think this is the school of the future?

Miriam: Yes – it's great!

What to do

The reporter has to write a short feature article based on this interview. Choose one of these headlines and then write an article of 100–120 words.

CRAZY SCHOOL WHERE
   ANYTHING GOES
SCHOOL FOR SOFTIES
SCHOOL OF THE FUTURE
TRIGWELL SCHOOL SHOWS THE
   WAY

TRIGWELL SCHOOL

PROSPECTUS

We have found that school rules are unnecessary. Each pupil is responsible for his/her own self-discipline in an atmosphere where adult, commonsense standards prevail. Acceptable behaviour, bearing in mind the needs of others, is recognised as the only requirement.

There is no prefect system, but some senior pupils volunteer to undertake various duties, which are organisational, rather than supervisory.

We believe that competition between pupils is unhealthy, unproductive and unnecessary. The best results are achieved when pupils seek to fulfil their own potential, regardless of the standards of others. For this reason all teaching groups are of mixed ability and there is no streaming, setting, or banding. Since each pupil is encouraged to match his/her own performance against previous personal achievements, there is no need for a system of rewards or punishments.

There are no school examinations, but each pupil's progress is closely monitored and a report card is issued each term, based on an assessment of that term's work, after consultation with the pupil.

There is no House system, since that can only be maintained in an atmosphere of rivalry. For the same reason we do not participate in inter-schools sports fixtures. We prefer to foster an atmosphere of enjoyment in extra-curricular, as in curricular, activities. Facilities are provided for an extensive range of leisure pursuits, with the emphasis always on the pleasure of personal involvement and self-improvement, rather than on the negative qualities of direct competition.

What to do

Writing

1   Make a list of the main differences between what is done in a traditional school and what is done at Trigwell.

Discussion

2   Explain in your own words the main ideas behind this policy.
3   Give your own views of these ideas: say which you think are good, and which are bad. In each case, give your reasons.
4   What would such ideas mean to the pupils at your school?

Typical fourth year timetables

At Trigwell

Mon	Maths	Careers Education	Information Technology	English
Tues	Science Today	Design Technology	English	French (Commercial)
Wed	Business Practice	Maths	Education for Leisure (Two different activities)	
Thurs	Design Technology	Business Practice	Maths	Information Technology
Fri	French (Conversation)	Science Today	English	Design Technology

At another local school

Mon	Maths	History	Geography	English
Tues	Physics and Chemistry	PE	English	French
Wed	Typing	Maths	Biology	Geography
Thurs	History	Typing	Maths	Games
Fri	French	Physics and Chemistry	English	Biology

What to do

1 Look at the Trigwell timetable: explain what you think each of the subjects (apart from English and Maths) will involve.
2 Explain what you think are the advantages and disadvantages of each of the two timetables for someone like you.
3 Make a list of the speakers on the opposite page. Alongside each name write down the timetable which you think that person would prefer and why.
4 Using your own school timetable, draw up your own *ideal* personal timetable, based on what you do now and what you would like to do. Remember to get the balance right and to include the 'compulsory' subjects (English, Maths).

Eric Simmons, MP

A school timetable has to be more realistic. It must reflect the needs of society. Schools have to look at the real world and meet the needs that they see.

Mrs Freeman, Head Teacher

From the fourth year, the timetable has to be tailored to the world of work. We'd love to keep the traditional subjects alongside the new ones, but there just isn't enough time in a week. You just have to decide on priorities and sadly this means that some subjects have to be dropped. Time will prove us right, I'm sure.

Jennie MacNamara, 15-year-old

It's fantastic! What's the point of learning lists of dates or where to the nearest millimetre a city is on the globe? We've got to be educated for tomorrow, and technology and commerce is what it's all about. Young people have got the future of the world in their hands, so let's make sure that the future is bright by giving them things to study that are really useful.

Mrs D Wilson, parent

Well, the timetable is certainly different from the one I did when I was at school. Most of the subjects I don't recognise at all. To be honest I'm not sure about it, but I am prepared to be advised by the professionals – after all, they are the experts. Still I sometimes wish that my Peter had a better background of general knowledge – you know, 1066, 1215, 1492 and all that.

Mrs M Crump, Owner of Traditional Groceries, Trigwell

I'm all for giving these young people a grounding in business, but we mustn't lose sight of our traditional values. You see falling standards everywhere you look these days. I believe in high standards and strong competition. That's what Britain's past prosperity was built on.

TV West News : Item 3

It has just been confirmed that Councillor Maurice Collins and Mrs Joan Freeman, Head Teacher of Trigwell School, will meet to discuss their differences at 2 o'clock this afternoon at the school.

Last week Councillor Collins launched an attack on the school at a Council meeting. He accused Trigwell School pupils of a lack of manners and an arrogant attitude. Councillor Collins laid the blame firmly on the school, and criticised a number of its policies.

In a letter to the Trigwell Times, Mrs Freeman defended the school and explained the thinking behind her attitude to education. She invited Councillor Collins to discuss with her any relevant issues, and today's meeting is the result of that invitation.

Councillor Collins has said that he is looking forward very much to putting his case to the Head Teacher. 'A meeting of this sort will suit me fine,' he said. He went on to say that he felt very strongly about the points he had made in the Council Chamber, and would be interested in the Head Teacher's response to particular cases he would be quoting.

Mrs Freeman declined to comment.

It is expected that a joint statement will be issued after the meeting.

Pair work: role-play

In this role-play, one person will be Councillor Collins and the other Mrs Freeman. (It doesn't matter whether the roles are played by boys or girls.) The activity is in three stages:

1 individual preparation
2 the discussion
3 preparing and writing a joint statement, or two statements.

Begin by deciding who will play each part.

Individual preparation: Councillor Collins

1 Read again what Councillor Collins has had to say so far.
2 Work out the answers to these questions:
   What sort of person is he?
   What is his attitude to the school?
   What does he think of the Head Teacher?
   How is he likely to behave at the meeting?
   What 'particular cases' (see page 26) will he mention?
3 Write a list of points he will want to make at the meeting. (You will need to look again at his statement on page 26 and Mrs Freeman's letter on page 27. Then add points of your own.)
4 Now spend some time thinking yourself into the part of Councillor Collins.

Individual preparation: Mrs Freeman

1 Read again what Mrs Freeman has had to say so far.
2 Work out the answers to these questions:
   What sort of person is she?
   What does she think of her school?
   What does she think of people who criticise her school?
   What is her attitude to Councillor Collins likely to be?
   How is she likely to behave at the meeting?
3 Write a list of the points she will want to make at the meeting. (You will need to look again at Councillor Collins' statement on page 26 and Mrs Freeman's letter on page 27. Then add points of your own.)
4 Now spend some time thinking yourself into the part of Mrs Freeman.

The discussion

When you are both ready, begin your discussion. Concentrate on staying in the role you have been given: only speak and behave in a way that you think is suitable for that role.

The statement

After your meeting write a short statement for radio and the press.
If you agree you can issue a joint statement.
If you fail to agree then each person should write their own statement, explaining why there is no agreement.

Writing

Think about, plan and write a piece of continuous writing on how you would organise an ideal school for the future. You should aim to deal with the following topics:

- regulations concerning the running of the school
- any specific rules
- uniform
- attendance at lessons
- staff/pupil relationships
- subjects to be studied
- attitudes to sport
- how the timetable would be planned, although there is no need to get too detailed about this

You can add points of your own which are not covered in this unit. For example:

- equipment and facilities which should be provided
- the length and timing of the school day
- the length of lessons
- the number and duration of breaks

Talking

As an individual, or as a member of a group, you can present your ideas about the ideal school as a talk. The topic is quite complicated and detailed, so you may find it useful to present some of the information in a **visual** form. For example:

a drawing of a suggested school uniform
a diagram to show how the school day is divided up
a large version of a new timetable
a plan of new classroom facilities

Coursework and spoken English

The writing you do when working on this page can be used for your coursework folder. The role-play on page 33 and the talk on this page could form part of your spoken English assessment.

Self-assessment

Look at the list of **English activities** on page 25. Use it as a guide to remind you of what you have covered. Write a brief assessment of your work on this unit:

- what you did
- what you found easy or difficult
- what you found interesting or boring
- what you think you did well
- areas where you need more practice
- what you think you learned from the unit
- your overall impression of the work

TV adaptation

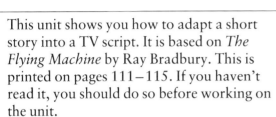

This unit shows you how to adapt a short story into a TV script. It is based on *The Flying Machine* by Ray Bradbury. This is printed on pages 111–115. If you haven't read it, you should do so before working on the unit.

Checklist

In this unit you will cover the following:

- **Preparing the story**
  recording your reactions to a story
  writing a summary of the storyline
- **Writing a scenario**
  listing the settings of a story
  dividing a story into scenes
  writing a scenario for a TV script
- **How a TV script works**
  learning how to set out a script for TV
- **Writing the script**
  turning part of a story into a script

The main stages

Preparing the story

Your reactions

Begin by making some notes on your thoughts
and feelings about the story. You could
include your views on any or all of these
points:

> what you think the story is *about* – its
> *message*;
> who the main characters are and what you
> think of them;
> where the story takes place and when;
> the atmosphere of the story;
> important moments in the story (these will
> often be the ones you remember best).

While you are doing this, you will probably
need to look at the story – or parts of it –
again, to remind yourself of things.

-It's about peace and what
rulers may have to do to
preserve it.

-The emperor is ruthless
but loves his country.

Writing the summary

You can now begin to make a summary of the
main events in the story. You will use this
when you come to write the scenario and,
later on, the script. A good way of doing this
is to use a **grid**, with one square for each event
in the story. Read the story again. As you
come to a new event, or something else
important in the story, fill in the next square
of the grid. This grid has been started for you.

The flying machine

In the year AD 400, the Emperor Yuan held his throne by the Great Wall of China, and the land was green with rain, readying itself towards the harvest, at peace, the people in his dominion neither too happy nor too sad.

Early on the morning of the first day of the first week of the second month of the new year, the Emperor Yuan was sipping tea and fanning himself against a warm breeze when a servant ran across the scarlet and blue garden tiles, calling, 'Oh, Emperor, Emperor, a miracle!'

'Yes,' said the Emperor, 'the air *is* sweet this morning.'

'No, no, a miracle!' said the servant, bowing quickly.

'And this tea is good in my mouth, surely that is a miracle.'

'No, no, Your Excellency.'

'Let me guess then – the sun has risen and a new day is upon us. Or the sea is blue. *That* now is the finest of all miracles.'

'Excellency, a man is flying!'

'What?' The Emperor stopped his fan.

'I saw him in the air, a man flying with wings. I heard a voice call out of the sky, and when I looked up there he was, a dragon in the heavens with a man in its mouth, a dragon of paper and bamboo, coloured like the sun and the grass.'

'It is early,' said the Emperor, 'and you have just wakened from a dream.'

'It is early, but I have seen what I have seen! Come, and you will see it too.'

'Sit down with me here,' said the Emperor. 'Drink some tea. It must be a strange thing, if it is true, to see a man fly. You must have time to think of it, even as I must have time to prepare myself for the sight.'

① The people are getting ready for harvest.	② They are peaceful and contented.	③ The Emperor is in the garden sipping tea.	④ The servant arrives with news.	⑤ At first the Emperor won't let him tell the news.
⑥ The servant tells him that he has seen a man flying.	⑦ At first the Emperor can't believe it.	⑧ Then he needs time to take it in.	⑨ They leave the garden and walk to the top of a hill.	⑩ The Emperor sees the man flying.

Writing the scenario

Now you can start to turn the **summary** into a **scenario**:

> A **summary** lists all the main events that the author put into the story.
> A **scenario** lists the main scenes, characters and actions that will be in the play.

1 The settings

The settings are the places where the action takes place. Copy and complete this list.

2 The scenes

The scenes are the main sections that the action is divided into. Usually a scene has only one setting. Mark the scenes on your summary grid like this:

3 The scenario

Now you are ready to write a detailed scenario. This includes the following information for each scene:

> the number of the scene
> the setting
> the characters in the scene
> the main events and conversations that take place

Use the pattern in this example and write the scenario for **three** other scenes in the story.

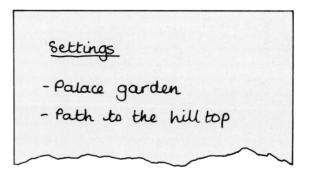

Settings

- Palace garden
- Path to the hill top

| ① The people are getting ready for harvest. | ② They are peaceful and contented. | ③ The Emperor is in the garden s... | ④ The servant arrives with news. | ⑤ At first the Emperor won't let him tell the news. |
| ⑥ The servant tells him that he has seen a man flying. | ⑦ At first the Emperor can't believe it. | ① | ⑨ They leave the garden and walk to the top of a hill. | ⑩ The Emperor sees the man flying. |

Scene: ④   Setting: Palace garden

Characters: Emperor, servant, Man, Guards

Main Events: - Emperor and man look at garden
- Emperor calls guards and tells them to arrest him.
- Emperor calls executioner.

Who uses the script?

The director

S/he is in charge of rehearsing and then recording the play. S/he decides not only how it should be acted, but what it should look like and how it should be filmed. So the director will use the script to give instructions to the cameraman.

The cameraman

The script should contain information about what the cameras should be doing. For example, it may be important that certain events should be seen in close-up.

The designer

The designer works with the director to make sure that the scenery and costumes are right for the play. S/he uses the script to understand when and where the play is set, and any practical problems that may be involved. So it should contain short descriptions of the different scenes, and important points about how the characters are dressed.

The actors

The actors interpret the play. They have:
- words to speak
- actions to perform.

The script must make these clear. It should also give them some idea of how the author sees each character.

How a TV script works

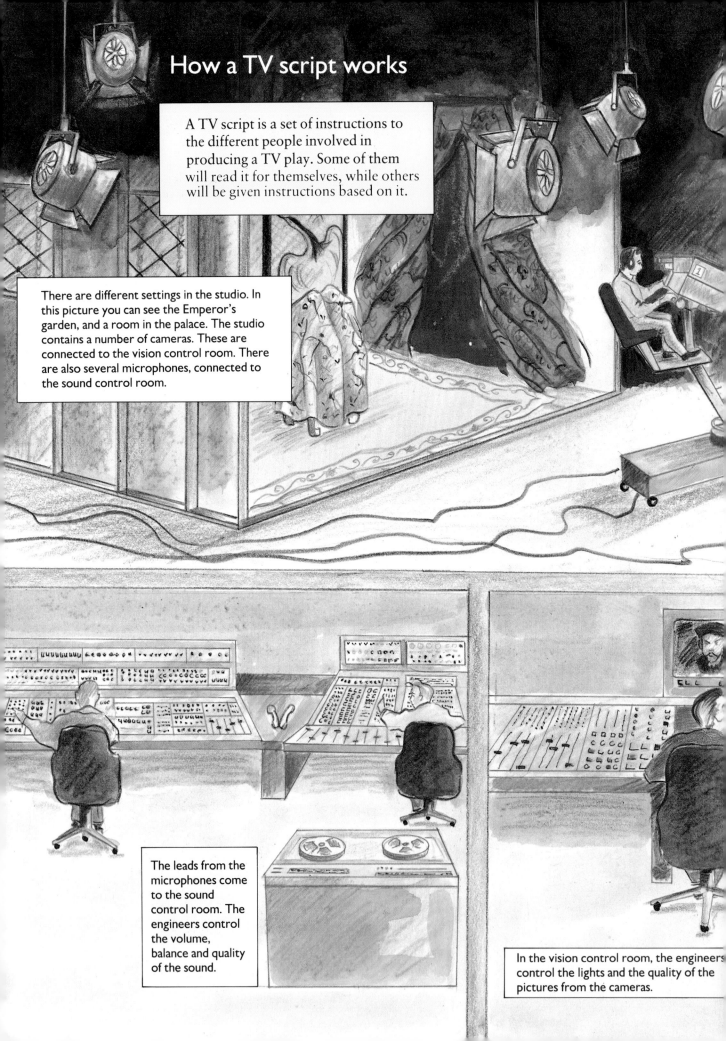

A TV script is a set of instructions to the different people involved in producing a TV play. Some of them will read it for themselves, while others will be given instructions based on it.

There are different settings in the studio. In this picture you can see the Emperor's garden, and a room in the palace. The studio contains a number of cameras. These are connected to the vision control room. There are also several microphones, connected to the sound control room.

The leads from the microphones come to the sound control room. The engineers control the volume, balance and quality of the sound.

In the vision control room, the engineers control the lights and the quality of the pictures from the cameras.

The stage manager makes sure that things are in the right place.

The floor manager links the director with all the people in the studio.

The director sits in the studio control room. S/he has a microphone by which s/he is in contact with all the people in the studio who are wearing headphones (cameramen, floor manager and others.) S/he also tells the vision mixer how the pictures from the different cameras should be used.

Writing the script

Now you can begin to write your script. Use
the scenario you wrote earlier, and choose
one of the scenes from it. Write the full script
for the scene you have chosen.

```
4. ENCLOSED PALACE GARDEN

EMPEROR : Call the executioner!                    (SERVANT HURRIES OFF.)


MAN : (BEWILDERED) What's this?  What have I done?

EMPEROR : Don't you know?

MAN : No.  What is it?

EMPEROR : (TO GUARDS) Here's a man who invents a machine and then asks us what he
has done!                                          (GUARDS LAUGH.)


MAN : I don't understand.

EMPEROR : No.  It's enough for you to invent the machine.  You don't bother to
think about why you have invented it...or what effect your invention will have.
                                                   (EXECUTIONER COMES TO THE DOOR AND
                                                    BOWS.)

EMPEROR : (TO EXECUTIONER) Make everything ready.
(TO MAN) Come with me.  I've got something I want you to see.

5. SMALL ROOM IN PALACE                            (EMPEROR ENTERS, FOLLOWED BY SERVANTS
                                                    AND MAN, HELD BY GUARDS.  EMPEROR GOES
                                                    TO A SMALL TABLE, COVERED BY A CLOTH.
                                                    HE SIGNS TO THE SERVANT, WHO REVEALS
                                                    THE MECHANICAL GARDEN.)


EMPEROR : There!

MAN : It is beautiful.
                                                   (EMPEROR PRESSES SMALL LEVER.  THE
EMPEROR : Now watch.                                MODEL SPRINGS INTO LIFE.)

                                                          the birds sing.
If you ask me what I have done, I can tell you.  I have made the
I've set the people walking, enjoying all the sights and sounds of the garden.

MAN : But that's just what I have done, too...


FILM:                                              MAN : I have found beauty.  I have
View of landscape from the air.                     flown on the moving wind.  I have
                                                    looked down on all the sleeping
The camera passes over houses and                   houses and gardens.  I have smelled
gardens and moves towards the                       the sea and even seen it, far beyond
distant sea.                                        the hills.


END FILM
```

42

What the script should contain

① The scene number and where the scene is set.

② A description of the actions that take place. (In capital letters and set to the right of the page so that they can be seen clearly.)

③ The name of each speaker. (In capital letters and underlined.)
④ The words spoken.

Developments

1   You can use this method to write other TV scene scripts:
     from another story in this book;
     from another story that you have read and that you like;
     from a story that you have written yourself;
     from an idea, or a set of characters, that you find interesting.

2   You can work with a group of people to act out a script that one of you has written: this way you find out whether the script works or not. If your school has video equipment, you can try recording part, or all, of a scene.

3   You can use the knowledge and experience you have gained to help you judge and comment on a TV drama. If you watch one that has been recorded, it will give you the opportunity to look at a particular scene more than once, to concentrate on how it is done.

Your folder

The writing you do in this unit could be used for the following purposes in a coursework folder:

1   Demonstrating understanding of a literary text.
2   Writing produced after studying a complete work of literature.
3   Writing in a controlled situation.

For all these you could submit a collection of **all** the writing done in the unit.

Self-assessment

Look at the **Checklist** on page 35. Use it as a guide to remind you of what you have covered. Write a brief assessment of your work on this unit:

- what you did
- what you found easy or difficult
- what you found interesting or boring
- what you think you did well
- areas where you need more practice
- what you think you learned from the unit
- your overall impression of the work

Olympic star

Jo – I'd like you to do a piece about Heather Eastwood for our 'famous athletes of the past' series. Theres a lot of interesting stuff about her in the files – I suggest you tackle the 'was she as bad as she was painted' line. 400 –500 words plus pix. OK?

PJr.

Sportsmad
MAGAZINE
NO. 25 £1.50

Inside ▶ DRUGS AT THE OLYMPICS
the truth behind the records
▶ GRAND PRIX round up
▶ PROTEIN all you need to know

SPORTSMAD MAGAZINE

Biography sheet

NAME ———————— Heather EASTWOOD
DATE OF BIRTH ——— 5/3/1950
EDUCATED ————— Morton Heath High School, Stockport 1961/4
Purton Secondary School, Barnsley 1964/6
EMPLOYMENT ——— Left school at 16 and took job as clerk at Lloyds Bank, Sheffield.

SPORTING
CAREER ————— Member AAA Junior team 1967
AAA National Championships 1969 - 2nd in 400m
Member AAA national team 1970, 1971
Olympic Games Munich 1972 - final 400m (2nd)
World record in 400m, Rome 1973
Unexpected and dramatic retirement October 1973

You are staff writer on *Sportsmad* magazine. You have been asked to write about Heather Eastwood, the famous British athlete. The unit contains the material you find as you are researching your article. At each stage you will find:

a) **Questions** to help you sort out what you think,
b) **Instructions** about making notes for your article.

Then, when you have gone through all the stages, you will be able to write the article.

English activities

The main English activities in this unit are:

- reading for information
- selecting and re-ordering information
- balancing different versions of the same character or event
- making notes
- writing a magazine article

Extract from Heather's letter to a young admirer

Dear Marion,

Sorry to hear that you don't like your new school. Still, cheer up, it can happen to anybody. I hated my first school. I got off to the worst possible start. I didn't like any of the teachers and I thought they'd all got it in for me. They said I didn't concentrate, I was wasting my time, I was stupid – and I believed them. So I just didn't try. There was only one teacher I got on with and that was Miss Pearson. She taught us history – or at least she tried to. But she also took the girls' athletics. She'd been county 200 metres champion at one time and she was super. I liked her so much I even tried at history! But even then, although I was only 12, I lived for athletics.

Extract from an interview with Miss James

Reporter: You used to be Head of Morton Heath High School, Heather Eastwood's first school?

Miss James: Yes.

Reporter: Do you remember her?

Miss James: Very well indeed.

Reporter: You must have a very good memory – after all it was many years ago, now.

Miss James: That's true, but there are good reasons.

Reporter: Yes? What are they?

Miss James: For one thing, she became a world famous athlete...

Reporter: And for another?

Miss James: ...I don't like speaking ill of people, even when it's all those years ago...

Reporter: But Heather Eastwood did leave your school rather suddenly, didn't she?

Miss James: Yes – I suppose it's no secret. She was an extremely **difficult** girl. There wasn't a teacher she got on with and she was always sulking and saying that people didn't understand her. And she had the most vicious temper when she was crossed. Oh yes, very difficult indeed.

Reporter: Can you give an example?

Miss James: Yes. There's one case that sticks in my mind. It was a games afternoon early in her second year...

Part of an interview with Heather Eastwood's mother

Interviewer: So Heather got on better at her new school in Yorkshire?

Mrs Eastwood: Oh yes. Definitely. She suddenly started getting good reports. She came home saying how nice all the teachers were...

Interviewer: And the athletics was still going well?

Mrs Eastwood: Yes. Of course she missed having Miss Pearson. But there again she was lucky. The teacher there –

Interviewer: Linda Marshall?

Mrs Eastwood: Yes, Mrs Marshall, that's right. She was a very highly-qualified coach. So Heather could continue with her running as if nothing had happened.

Interviewer: By now she'd moved up from the 200 metres to the 400. Is that right?

Mrs Eastwood: Yes. I think she'd really only stuck to the 200 to please Miss Pearson, because she was a 200 metres runner. Then Mrs Marshall showed her how much stronger she could be at 400 metres, and she never looked back.

Interviewer: Why did Heather leave school at 16?

Mrs Eastwood: She found school rather restricting – thought the teachers were a bit narrow-minded. And she wanted to be able to devote herself to her running.

Interviewer: But she had to get a job?

Mrs Eastwood: Oh yes. You see we've never been well off...

What to do

Questions

1 What did Heather think of her first school?
2 What impression did her first Head have of her?
3 What kind of thing do you think happened on that games afternoon?
4 What would you want to ask Miss James to find out more about Heather's life at Morton Heath?
5 Does the interview with Heather's mother help you to understand why Heather wasn't happy at her first school?
6 What additional information does the second interview give that helps you understand Heather as a person?
7 Are there any further questions you would like to ask Heather's mother?
8 What are **your** impressions of what Heather was like at school, and what are they based on?

Instructions

The first part of your article will be about **Heather's schooldays**. You need to take a clear line on **how** Heather behaved, as well as describing what she did. You can probably only allow 75 – 100 words for this.

1 Make a list of the main **facts** you need to include.
2 Make a list of the main **impressions** you want to convey about Heather's attitude to school.

Problems

Extract from a letter from Mr Stimpson

At the time Heather Eastwood was working as a clerk for Lloyds Bank Sheffield, I was Assistant Manager in charge of staffing. As far as I can remember she was a pleasant, hardworking girl who never caused any problems. She got on well with people. I'm afraid I can't remember much else about her at all.

I'm sorry I can't help you further.

Yours sincerely,

R. Stimpson

Extracts from Heather's diary for 1969

TUESDAY 14 JUNE

Another row with Mr Stimpson today. He can't understand why I need to take time off for training. I said I didn't mind him stopping my pay, so long as I could come in an hour late each morning after training. (I have to get up at half past five anyway). He said that wouldn't make any difference. It was the principle of the thing. I don't see why – none of the other girls mind, because I've asked them. Anyway I've got to concentrate on my training for the next week and a half. Then it's the AAA championship. I'd worry about stupid old Stimpson after that!

THURSDAY 30 JUNE

Stimpson told me today I was on positively my last chance – stupid old _ _ _ _! Anyway all the girls told me how pleased they were I'd done so well in the Nationals...

Anonymous phone call

While you are writing up the second section of the article, you receive an anonymous telephone call. This is part of it.

Caller: I suppose you know that she was more or less kicked out of her first school –

Reporter: Morton Heath High School?

Caller: Yes. She was so unpopular with all the teachers – and most of the kids – that she was asked to leave.

Reporter: But I thought her father got a new job in Barnsley.

Caller: That was after – when he knew that they were going to have to take her away from the school anyway.

Reporter: Why did the teachers dislike her so much?

Caller: She was Miss High-and-Mighty, wasn't she? And I'll tell you another thing. That school wasn't the only place she got thrown out of.

Reporter: No? Where else?

Caller: Lloyds Bank Sheffield – that's where else.

Reporter: I thought she left voluntarily.

Caller: That's what they **said** but it wasn't what happened, was it?

Reporter: Wasn't it?

Caller: No. They told her that if she didn't leave they'd give her the sack.

Reporter: Why?

Caller: Same reason – she was so big-headed. Used to turn up half-way through the morning or even later and then act as if she was the manager, instead of an ordinary junior clerk.

Reporter: Look – who are you? How do you know all this?

(*At this point the Caller rang off.*)

Extracts from Heather's diary for 1970

> **SUNDAY 7 AUGUST**
>
> I feel much happier now I've left the bank. I know Mum's worried about making ends meet, but I'm sure it'll be all right. Now I've definitely been selected for the international match in Zagreb, I feel really confident. Anyway I'm bound to stand a better chance of a job after that.

> **SUNDAY 21 AUGUST**
>
> Zagreb
> Fantastic! First in the 400 metres, in spite of the terrible weather. No problems at all, except for that East German girl, Helga Seidler, who nearly caught me at the end. But that Mamie Harris they made all the fuss about - she had to struggle to make third place. Afterwards everyone was so nice. I rang Mum and she was over the moon.

What to do

Questions

1 There are three different versions of what happened at the bank: Heather's, Mr Stimpson's, and that of the anonymous caller. What are the main differences between them?

2 How can you decide which one is right?

3 On this page there is information about two areas of Heather's life:
   a) her work at the bank
   b) her sporting achievements
   How will you balance these two in this part of your article?

Instructions

The second part of your article will be about **Heather's rise to the top.** You need to decide how you are going to balance out the different stories about Heather's life. You can probably allow about 100–150 words for this.

1 Make a list of the main **facts** you need to include.

2 Make a list of the main **impressions** you want to convey about this part of Heather's life.

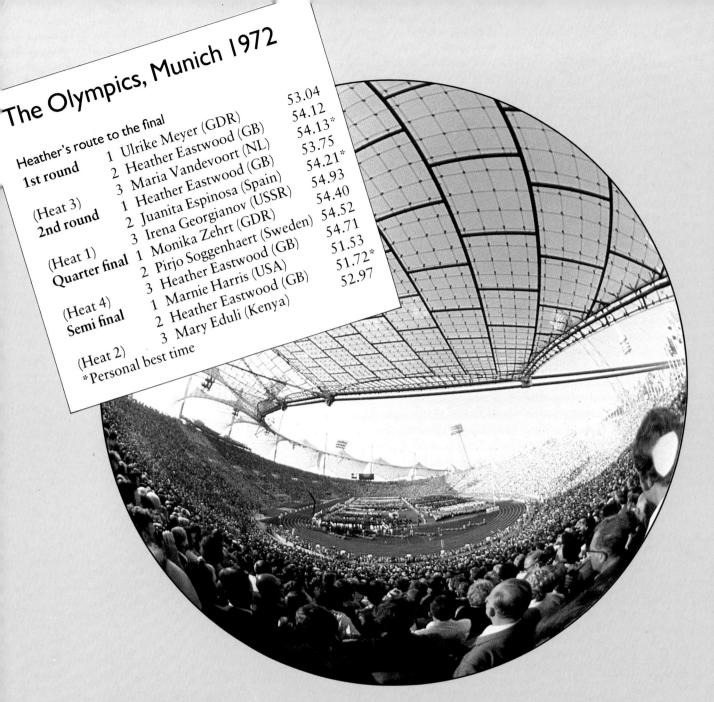

The Olympics, Munich 1972

Heather's route to the final

1st round	1	Ulrike Meyer (GDR)	53.04
	2	Heather Eastwood (GB)	54.12
	3	Maria Vandevoort (NL)	54.13*
(Heat 3)			
2nd round	1	Heather Eastwood (GB)	53.75
	2	Juanita Espinosa (Spain)	54.21*
	3	Irena Georgianov (USSR)	54.93
(Heat 1)			
Quarter final	1	Monika Zehrt (GDR)	54.40
	2	Pirjo Soggenhaert (Sweden)	54.52
	3	Heather Eastwood (GB)	54.71
(Heat 4)			
Semi final	1	Marnie Harris (USA)	51.53
	2	Heather Eastwood (GB)	51.72*
	3	Mary Eduli (Kenya)	52.97
(Heat 2)			

*Personal best time

Heather at Munich

The person who really amazed everybody in the women's team was Heather Eastwood. I'd heard from one or two people that she could be a bit moody and difficult, but it wasn't like that at all. I arranged that she shared rooms with Winnie Stanford, the discus thrower, because I knew Winnie was a person who could get on with almost anyone. But as soon as Heather got to the Olympic village, her eyes lit up and she became the life and soul of the party. It was as if this was the moment in her life she'd been living for. As for her performance on the track – that's history now. She came out as very much the second string and she just amazed everyone. It was only because of that unfortunate incident on the final bend that she didn't win the final and take the Olympic record as well.

from *Front Runner* (The autobiography of Ellen Deane, Manager of the British Women's team in 1972)

Result of women's 400 metres

1 Monika Zehrt 51.08 (new Olympic record)
2 Heather Eastwood 51.39 (personal best)
3 Marnie Harris 52.13

Extracts from the race commentary

. . . . and Heather Eastwood has got a fantastic start. She's already two yards up on Ulrike Meyer . . . . now as they go into the back straight it's Heather Eastwood for Great Britain in with a real chance. It's between her and Marnie Harris, with Monika Zehrt close behind. As they come into the final bend, it's Heather Eastwood about half a yard up on Marnie Harris, and I think she's going to hold on . . . . and now what's happened? It looks as though there's been a collision . . . . . . Heather Eastwood has stumbled and so has Marnie Harris . . . . and Monika Zehrt has stormed into the lead. And she has won! What a fantastic and controversial finish ! . . . .
. . . . . I still don't exactly know what happened, but it looks as if Marnie Harris began to stray towards the inner line of her lane, and this made Heather Eastwood move across to keep out of her way and she must have hit her foot on the kerb that runs round the inside of the track. She recovered her balance, but not in time to keep her lead. But the judges decided that in fact Marnie Harris did **not** cross the line, so she kept third place, and poor Heather Eastwood had to be content with the silver medal.

What they said after the race

Heather Eastwood

Marnie Harris was moving across into my lane. I could see her out of the corner of my eye the whole time. She's never forgiven me for beating her at Zagreb . . . . I felt her crowding me out and I must have moved away just enough to hit the kerb as we were coming into the last straight.

Marnie Harris

Of course I didn't cross into her lane: she was pushing into **my** lane all the way round the last bend. If you look at the video of the final you can see that she's drifting out all the way round that bend. The thing is: she was tiring fast – that's why she touched the kerb. I don't like to say this, but that British girl is just a bad loser.

Questions

Again there are two sides to this part of Heather's story.

1 How do Ellen Deane's comments fit in with what you know so far?
2 What do **you** think happened in the final of the 400 metres?

Instructions

Now make notes for this part of your article. You need to deal with:

1 Heather's unexpected success in getting into the final,
2 What Ellen Deane says about how she behaved,
3 What happened in the final.

How the story ends

You should now have notes on Heather's career up to the end of 1972. They should allow you to write about 300–350 words of your article. This means that you can write 50–150 words more about the rest of her career.

1   Look at the biography sheet on page 1. Bearing in mind what you know so far, what do you think happened?
2   Make some notes about what you think might have happened in 1973.

Writing the article

You can now use your notes as the basis of your article. It should have these main sections:

1   Heather's school life
2   Early problems and successes
3   The Olympic Games
4   How her athletic career ended

Coursework

The work you do on this unit can be used in an English coursework folder. It covers the following areas of the syllabus:

- reading and understanding non-literary material
- writing in response to non-literary material
- writing in a 'closed' situation/directed writing

Self-assessment

Look at the list of **English activities** on page 45. Use it as a guide to remind you of what you have covered. Write a brief assessment of your work on this unit:

- what you did
- what you found easy or difficult
- what you found interesting or boring
- what you think you did well
- areas where you need more practice
- what you think you learned from the unit
- your overall impression of the work

Autobiography

A lot of the writing you do is autobiographical: in one way or another it is about **you**. You may also have read autobiographical writing by other people. This unit shows you different ways in which you can write about your own life. It leads to the production of your own anthology of autobiographical writing.

Year	Age	Details particular to you	Life changes / landmarks	Important events
1987	14-15	Secondary school - 4th year of Beverley School	Sprained my foot - X ray at Kingston Hospital.	Watched cup final.
1986	13-14	3rd year of Beverley School.	Holiday in Spain - first time abroad.	World cup. Westland affair.
1985	12-13	2nd year of Beverley school.	Moved house.	Boris Becker won at Wimbledon.
1984	11-12	1st year of Beverley School.	Got school uniform for Beverley School.	Harrods bombing.
1983	10-11	Primary school - 4th year of Malden Manor.	Nan died.	
1982	9-10	3rd year of Malden Manor.	Went	
1981	8-9	2nd year of Malden Manor.	wedd... Holid...	
1980	7-8	1st year of Malden Manor.	went t... Joined	
	6-7	4th year of infant school.		
	5-6	3rd year of infant school.	learnt t...	
	-5	2nd year of infant school.	Sister Samantha born.	
	4	1st year of infant school.	First day at sc...	
		Play group		
			Given a pet c... as a Christ...	
			Born 18...	

HE WAS SLIM WITH BROWN HAIR AND BLUE EYES HE WORE A SPOTTED SHIRT AND HAD HIS TRUSTY DOG "FANG" WITH HIM.

Who am I?

1 Look at the chart below and think about how each of the factors listed has influenced you and affected the person you are.

2 Make up a chart of your own.

3 Make a few notes on each of the factors on the chart.

4 How do your notes compare with those other people have made?

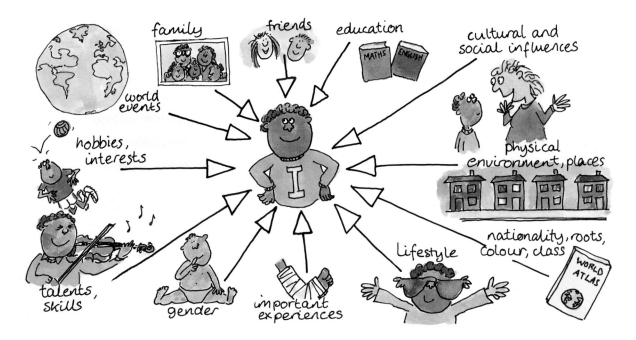

Now it's time to look at things from the opposite point of view. What influence do **you** have on the outside world?

1 Look at the chart below and think how you have influenced each person or thing listed.

2 Make up a chart of your own.

3 Make notes on each of the factors in the chart.

4 How do your notes compare with those other people have made?

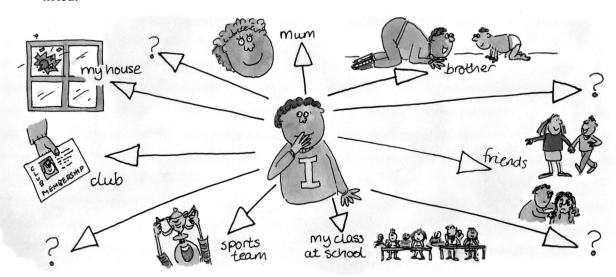

Life chart

A good way of recording the main stages in your life is to make a **life chart**. When you want to choose which parts of your life to write about in more detail, you can use it to help you decide.

1   Look at the example on this page. Think about the **important** events and memories that you want to include in your chart.

2   Copy the outline of the chart.
3   Fill in the columns for your life.

Warning: if you want to keep parts of your life private, don't put them on your chart – or keep a private version that you don't show to other people!

Year	Age	Details particular to you	Life changes / landmarks	Important events
1987	14–15	Secondary school –	Sprained my foot – X ray at Kingston Hospital.	Watched cup final.
1986	13–14	4th year of Beverley School.		World cup. Westland affair.
1985	12–13	3rd year of Beverley School.	Holiday in Spain – first time abroad.	Boris Becker won at Wimbledon.
1984	11–12	2nd year of Beverley School.	Moved house.	Harrods bombing.
1983	10–11	1st year of Beverley School.	Got school uniform for Beverley School.	
1982	9–10	Primary school – 4th year of Malden Manor.	Nan died.	General Election.
1981	8–9	3rd year of Malden Manor.		Falklands war
1980	7–8	2nd year of Malden Manor.	Went to Aunty Jo's wedding.	
1979	6–7	1st year of Malden Manor.	Holiday in Blackpool - went to the fair. Joined cubs.	
1978	5–6	4th year of infant school.		Olympics in Moscow.
1977	4–5	3rd year of infant school.	Learnt to swim.	
1976	3–4	2nd year of infant school.	Sister Samantha born.	
1975	2–3	1st year of infant school.	First day at school.	
1974	1–2	Play group		
1973	1		Given a pet cat, Tinsel, as a Christmas present.	
1972			Born 18.7.72	

I remember . . . we remember . . .

One of the things that helps us know who we are is the memories we share
with other people: family
         friends
         people in our locality

I remember seeing 'Bambi'.
I remember 'fresh' meaning 'good'.
I remember Jimmy Osmond and 'Long-Haired-Lover-From-Liverpool' on Top-of-the-Pops.
I remember leg-warmers.
I remember 'Star Wars' — amazing!
I remember the 'Magic Roundabout' and Zebedee.
I remember Shergar being stolen for ransom.
I remember watching Tizwas and Swapshop.
I remember English, Irish and Scottish jokes told in the garage.
I remember Sindy and Barbie dolls.
I remember Tiny Tears.
I remember home computers.
I remember digital watches.
I remember the Falklands and the sinking of the Belgrano.
I remember fingerless gloves and pedal-pushers — bright green.
I remember the Brighton bombing.
I remember Mrs T being elected — HELP!
I remember Channel 4 starting — Una Stubbs did the ad.
I remember Breakfast Time.
I remember soap operas — Eastenders.
I remember riots in Toxteth, Brixton and St Paul's.

I remember J.R. being shot.
I remember when Bobby came back from the dead!
I remember when Ian Botham was charged with taking drugs.
I remember AIDS.
I remember the Miners' Strike.
I remember seeing Doctor Who.
I remember seeing Watership Down—dead frightening.
I remember 101 Dalmations.
I remember ABBA.
I remember long party dresses and long springs coming out of heads.
I remember skateboarding.
I remember the wounding of Sefton in the Hyde Park bombing.
I remember roller-skating.
I remember the very hot summer of '76.
I remember Charles and Di being married.
I remember John Lennon being shot.
I remember the lifting of the Mary Rose.
I remember the Iranian hostages.
I remember the new exam — GCSE.
I remember Cecil Parkinson and Sarah Keays.
I remember Heseltine and Brittan resigning over Westland Affair.

Group work: brainstorming

1 Every person in the group has a piece of paper and a pen.
2 For **exactly** three minutes, everybody says all the things they can remember about the time in which they have lived:
   pop   the weather
   politics   TV
   world events words and sayings
   fashions   . . . anything . . .

3 Everybody writes everything down.
4 Nobody comments, makes noises, stops for a chat.
5 After three minutes, stop and read through what you have written.
6 Discuss your list and add to it.
7 Write the list out so that you – and other people – can understand it.

Memory triggers

We are often reminded of past experiences by everyday sights, smells, sounds, textures. Something triggers off a memory and we suddenly have a clear picture of something we may not have thought about for years.

> Staring at a blank piece of paper
> Blank walls
> My life was blank then
> No family, a few friends
>
> I couldn't see a good life ahead
> Only Life forcing me to grow up
> Perhaps I didn't want to
> So much fighting!
>
> I have no family
> No home base
> I'm a live-in lodger . . .
> But I have to survive
> My family is at school
>
> I am 15 years old
> Or am I 20 inside?
> Outside I appear 10 but that isn't me
> It's an act
>
> I deceive everyone
> I live a lie
> I am 20 years old with a hole in my life
>
> I rely on my friends
> To give me love and support
> If they reject me
> If they turn against me
> I will be again
> A blank piece of paper.

Solo work: speed writing

1 Look around you now until you find something to focus on which triggers a memory. It may be a person, a colour, a picture, the view outside . . . anything.
2 Write rapidly to try to capture the memory.
3 If necessary, try again.
4 When you are satisfied that you have captured something worthwhile, you can begin to shape and polish your memory.

Describing yourself

Work with a partner → Write notes on what s/he looks like → Discuss them → Make notes on his / her personality →

1 Pair work

For this activity, you need to work with a partner, preferably one whom you can trust to be fair and honest. You are going to write two accurate and truthful descriptions:

of your partner,
of yourself as others see you.

2 Physical description

Start by making notes about what your partner looks like. Cover these topics, and any others you can think of:

height/weight/build
colour of hair/eyes
complexion
shape and appearance of face
typical expression and posture
typical clothing
other features that mark him/her out

3 Consultation

When you have finished, read your notes to your partner. Discuss points of disagreement. If you think your partner is wrong, try to persuade him/her to change what s/he has written. Make any changes you think necessary.

4 Personality

Now make notes on your partner's personality. Cover these topics, and any others you can think of:

interests
talents
moods
behaviour towards other people
good and bad points
strengths and weaknesses

Discuss them

Write up your description

Discuss it

Describe yourself as someone else might see you.

5 Consultation

When you have finished, show your notes to your partner. Discuss points of disagreement. If you think your partner is wrong, try to persuade him/her to change what s/he has written. Make any changes you think necessary.

6 Writing up

Use the notes you have got to write a detailed description of your partner.

7 Comments

When you have finished, show each other what you have written and read it carefully. **On your own paper,** write your comments on what your partner has written about you.

8 Your turn

Now write a description and character study of **yourself,** but in the third person – that is as if it was someone else who was writing about you. Use 'he' or 'she', rather than 'I'. Go through exactly the same stages as you did before, commenting on each other's work.

Ghost writing

Many published autobiographies by famous people are in fact written not by them but by professional writers. This is known as **ghost writing**. The famous person talks about his or her life with the ghost writer, and perhaps writes some notes. The ghost writer then does further research, using letters, diaries, and press cuttings. S/he may also interview friends and relatives to add interesting details and give the story more human interest.

You are now going to do some ghost writing. You will need to work with a partner. Each person will act as ghost writer for the other.

On your own

1 Choose one part of your life to describe to your partner. Choose from the life chart you made earlier, or take one of these:
   - your first week at secondary school
   - the best (or worst) week of your life
   - a high point in your school career
   - a holiday you like to remember (or forget)

2 Write fairly detailed notes for your partner about this time in your life.

3 Collect photos, diaries, letters, postcards, scrapbooks and anything else which might be useful.

4 Give your partner the notes and material you have collected.

5 Study the notes and material your partner has given you.
6 Make a list of questions to ask and information you will need before you can start writing.

Working together

7 Decide who will be the writer and who will be the subject.
8 The writer now talks to his subject about the time in question.

Writer
Use the list of questions you have prepared, but add to them when necessary. Your aim is to be able to write about your partner with real understanding. You need to know his/her feelings at the time, as well as exactly what happened. Decide what further research or information you now need. Remember to make full notes at each stage.

Subject
Give the writer as much information as possible. Answer his/her questions as fully as you can.

9 Now swap over and repeat 8.
10 Write the first draft. (Don't forget that you are a ghost writer, pretending to be the subject, so write as 'I'.)
11 Show the first draft to your partner. Discuss it with him/her. Get your partner's advice on how it could be improved.
12 Write a second draft.

Third person

On the last two pages you wrote about someone else as if you were them. Now you are going to write about yourself as if you were someone else.

You will have to talk about yourself as 'he' or 'she', not 'I'.

What to do

1 Choose one moment, event, experience in your life, which you feel is important. Perhaps it is something which has influenced the way you are now. (You may find it helps to look again at your life chart.)

2 Spend some time thinking and jotting down notes about the experience. Include both how you felt about it at the time and how you feel about it now.

3 Make more careful notes about:
the order in which things happened (and the period of time),
the people involved,
where it happened (and the surroundings),
how this experience has influenced you,
what you would like the reader to understand about you from reading about the experience.

4 Write a first draft. Write fast. Don't stop too much to think. Write as 'he' or 'she'.

5 Show this draft to someone else whose advice you trust. Listen carefully to their comments and think about what you have written.

6 Write your second draft.

These pieces of writing were done by pupils of Nailsea School, Avon, as part of their work on autobiography.

The sun reflected painfully off the rich, blue ocean. It warmed the two children who were playing outside a house built on stilts. They were crouched in the dry dusty soil, surrounded by gathered pebbles, leaves and flowers. Laughing, they put crimson Hibiscus trumpets in their hair, threaded cream and yellow Frangi Pangi flowers onto string and made the bright orange 'bird' flowers squawk. The pebbles and leaves soon became a beautiful garden, and the dry grasses became children. For hours they sat acting out adventures. Neither one noticed that the other's skin was a different colour from their own.

The White girl, now much older, sits watching the St Paul's race riot on television, wishing the world could be as innocent as those two children playing in the sun.

That morning came for him. The weekend was over now and he had to get ready for school. He put on his clothes and then reached up and took the glasses' case off the shelf. As he opened the case the smell of the optician's house hit him in the face. During his breakfast he thought about what they would say or do. He munched down the last spoon of Cornflakes and helped it down with a gulp of tea. He opened the door and his Mum said,'Don't worry, you'll be all right.'He replied with a gentle nod and shut the door with a prolonged slam. He dragged himself up the garden path, crossed over the main road and up to the side-gate of his school. It was easy for him

because his school was only up the road. He heard the soft voice of the optician going through his mind again. 'They suit you, they suit you,' he heard echoing in and out of his mind. He went into school and walked up to the foot of the steps which led up to the noisy class room. He saw that a few of his friends were in, and the girls creeping around the teacher as they normally did on Monday mornings. He went up to the door and opened it; he did not look at them as his heart went Bang, Bang, Bang. His brain felt as if it was getting bigger and bigger. Then suddenly it all stopped. The teacher looked round and said to him,'I like your glasses, David. They look nice on you.'His reply was a gentle nod of his head,

followed by dropping himself down on a chair near his friends. No-one seemed to notice, he thought. They would have been in fits of laughter by now but his friends just said things which kind of made him feel proud of having his glasses on. Even the girls did not say anything nasty - only things like the lads had said to him before. A few days went past and after that no-one seemed even to know he had them on in the first place. He still got a few not so nice comments from some of the older pupils in the school but he did not take any notice and they soon found someone else to pick on. Afterwards he wondered what he had got so worried and up-tight about, but it was all in the past for him now.

Developments

Your autobiography anthology

You should now have several pieces of writing to include in an anthology of autobiographical writing. This could form part of your folder of coursework. Here are a few more suggestions for writing to complete your anthology.

1   Write one or more poems about yourself. You could use the **memory trigger** idea (on page 57) to start you off.
2   Write about a friend, or relative, or someone else who has been important in your life.
3   Write one of the following:

    a history of my life as a reader
    a history of my life as a TV viewer
    a history of my life as a pop music listener
    a history of my life as a pupil

In each case describe your earliest experiences and how your interests, tastes and behaviour have changed.

4   Write about the **places** which have been most important to you. These could include: homes, parks, schools, beaches, woods, holiday sites, shopping-centres, sports grounds, etc.
5   Look back over all the work you have done for this project. Think again about the things which have influenced your life. Think about what has helped shape the person you are now. Write a longer piece entitled, *Why I am who I am.*

Evaluation

Look at the writing you have done in this unit. Think about everything you have done: thinking, talking, research. Write a short self-evaluation of your work. Include:

● what you did best
● what you enjoyed most
● what you learned most from
● whether the unit has helped you understand yourself and the world you live in any better
● any other comments

Save our village!

MAP OF PROPOSED DEVELOPMENT

(Map labels:) TO HEREFORD · B 3128 · EXISTING VILLAGE OF WYEDEAN · RIVERSIDE BUSINESS PARK (PROPOSED) · RIVERSIDE HOUSING DEVELOPMENT (PROPOSED) · RIVER WYE · 0 — ½ K

Deighton Developments

PRESS RELEASE

RIVERSIDE BUSINESS PARK

AN EXCITING NEW BUSINESS OPPORTUNITY! A NEW DEAL FOR WYEDEAN!

Deighton Developments announce a bold and exciting new plan for the West of England. In association with its sister company Deighton Investments, the Company plans to develop a 100-acre site on the edge of Wyedean, Hereford & Worcester.

... of 62 acres, will be developed as a high ... size from 500 square feet ... of businesses

---

Radical Action for a Green Environment

PRESS RELEASE

RIVERSIDE VANDALISM!

Deighton Developments, a London-based property company, ... desecrate one of the most beautiful areas of the Wye Val... progress – by which they mean maximum profit ... 100 acres of beautiful water meadows a... turn them into an industrial ... The fields, known loc... farmed them for cen... offer a unit... but...
said... Deve... can'... this... Loca... public... both be... Forme... number... Norfolk... intends to... list.

RIVERSIDE VANDALS

This beautiful stretch of the Wye Valley is now under threat from vandalism! Property tycoon Barry Deighton, of Deighton Developments says he intends to build a 100-acre business park and housing scheme on a stretch of prime agricultural land along the River Wye, just outside the picturesque village of Wyedean.

It is well known that Deighton Developments have been looking for some time for a suitable site to build an American-style hi-tech business park in the west

of England. Deighton's business associate Anne Marlowe told me today that she aims to make the Wye Valley Britain's answer to the American Silicone Valley. 'It has excellent communications, being close to the M50 and the M5. You can be in London in just over two hours and Birmingham in one and a half. It's a beautiful place and people will come a long way to work here. The project will bring a lot of employment to the area.'

Local people are outraged at

the idea. Diana Searle, Chairperson of the Wyedean Parish Council, said, 'This is one of the most beautiful parts of England. It has been designated an Area of Outstanding Natural Beauty. This project is nothing short of vandalism. It's pure greed on the part of the landowner and the developer.'

The property owner whose sale of the land started this whole thing off, ex-farmer and local businessman Mostyn Grummer, was not available for comment.

This unit is about a planning problem. You will be asked to look at it from different points of view and then talk and write about the issues involved.

English activities

The unit gives practice in these activities:

- pair discussion
- role-play
- group discussion
- group presentation of an argument
- making notes
- writing: a speech presenting an argument, an article, a diary entry

- presenting information in a variety of media: newspaper report, press release, script, pictures, maps
- detailed understanding of a text
- preparing and expressing an argument

RIVERSIDE VANDALS

This beautiful stretch of the Wye Valley is now under threat from vandalism! Property tycoon Barry Deighton, of Deighton Developments says he intends to build a 100-acre business park and housing scheme on a stretch of prime agricultural land along the River Wye, just outside the picturesque village of Wyedean.

It is well known that Deighton Developments have been looking for some time for a suitable site to build an American-style hi-tech business park in the west of England. Deighton's business associate Anne Marlowe told me today that she aims to make the Wye Valley Britain's answer to the American Silicone Valley. 'It has excellent communications, being close to the M50 and the M5. You can be in London in just over two hours and Birmingham in one and a half. It's a beautiful place and people will come a long way to work here. The project will bring a lot of employment to the area.'

Local people are outraged at the idea. Diana Searle, Chairperson of the Wyedean Parish Council, said, 'This is one of the most beautiful parts of England. It has been designated an Area of Outstanding Natural Beauty. This project is nothing short of vandalism. It's pure greed on the part of the landowner and the developer.'

The property owner whose sale of the land started this whole thing off, ex-farmer and local businessman Mostyn Grummer, was not available for comment.

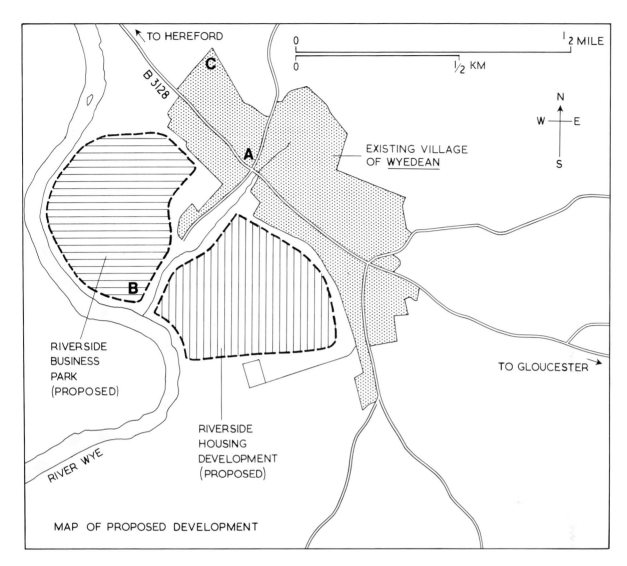

Map labels:
TO HEREFORD
B 3128
C
0 — 2 MILE
0 — ½ KM
N W E S
A
EXISTING VILLAGE OF WYEDEAN
B
RIVERSIDE BUSINESS PARK (PROPOSED)
TO GLOUCESTER
RIVER WYE
RIVERSIDE HOUSING DEVELOPMENT (PROPOSED)
MAP OF PROPOSED DEVELOPMENT

Reading and note-making

1 What are your immediate reactions to the situation? Make written notes on your opinion and the reasons for it.
2 On the map are marked the homes of three residents of Wyedean, A, B, and C. How do you think each of these might feel about the development? What will affect their opinions? Make written notes on each one.

Oral work: pairs

1 Discuss your notes with a partner.
   or
2 Make up a conversation about the development. Choose one of the following pairs of characters. (It doesn't matter whether the parts are played by boys or girls: it's the **opinions and attitudes** that matter.
   Anne Marlowe and Diana Searle
   Anne Marlowe and B
   B and C
   A and C

The truth about Mostyn Grummer

News of the proposed development and the strong feelings on both sides has brought the press to Wyedean. Many of the reporters are very interested in the mystery man of the whole affair: Mostyn Grummer. He is the owner of Grummer's Meadows and stands to make a huge profit if the Riverside development goes ahead. But nobody knows anything about him. He is a widower and lives alone in a huge house in Hereford. He is rarely seen in public and likes to keep himself to himself. Recently, however, rumours about Mostyn Grummer and about 'what he gets up to in that big house of his' have begun to circulate. Two local reporters have begun to collect information about him: Iain Mackay of *The County Times* and 'Digger Treadwell' of the *Dean Weekly News*. *The County Times* is a respectable and well-known local weekly. The *Dean Weekly News* is a new free advertising paper that specialises in scandal.

Interview between Mostyn Grummer and Iain Mackay

Mackay: It's good of you to see me Mr Grummer.

Grummer: That's all right. What do you want?

Mackay: I was hoping you would give me an interview.

Grummer: For the television?

Mackay: No, for my newspaper, *The Times*.

Grummer: What do you want to know?

Mackay: You are one of the central characters in the Riverside Development Enquiry, and I'd like to get some background information about you. There are so many rumours flying around at the moment –

Grummer: I know, I know. You don't have to tell me. I'm fed up with the whole business. It's in the hands of my solicitors.

Mackay: Can you tell me Mr Grummer what line of business you are in? I know that you made a handsome profit when you sold the main part of your farm in 1981.

Grummer: What if I did? It was my farm and I had the right to sell it, whatever village people said.

Mackay: And what did you do with the money?

Grummer: Not that it's any of your business, but I invested it.

Mackay: In what?

Grummer: Property mostly. I started a business buying up ruined cottages in Wales, doing them up as holiday homes and then selling them again. Very profitable it turned out, too.

Mackay: And what about these rumours about income tax and the police?

Grummer: Mostly a pack of lies. I had a slight disagreement with the tax man about how much I owed him, but that was all settled years ago. And I have never been in any kind of trouble with the law. And if you say I have, I'll sue you for every penny you've got!

Mackay: And what about these rumours about your private life?

Grummer: I'm not answering any questions about that. In fact I'm not answering any more questions at all. Good day to you.

What to do

As you can see, there are two journalists preparing a story about Mostyn Grummer. Each has a separate set of information. Neither has access to the information of the other. Both can choose from the same set of three photographs. Write the report that each one sends to his/her paper. Choose one photograph for each and explain why you have chosen it.

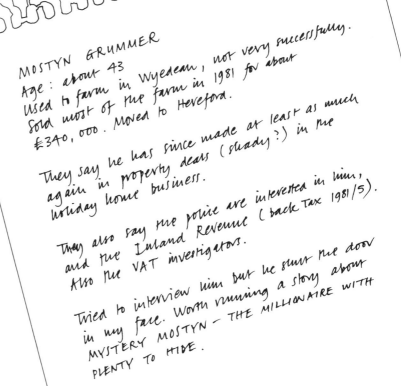

IF YOU WANT TO KNOW ABOUT MOSTYN GRUMMER ARSK HIM ABOUT IS FANCY WOMEN WHAT HE KEEPS IN IS HOUSE

MOSTYN GRUMMER
Age: about 43
Used to farm in Wyedean, not very successfully.
Sold most of the farm in 1981 for about £340,000. Moved to Hereford.

They say he has since made at least as much again in property deals (shady?) in the holiday home business.

They also say the police are interested in him, and the Inland Revenue (back Tax 1981/5). Also the VAT investigators.

Tried to interview him but he slam the door in my face. Worth running a story about MYSTERY MOSTYN — THE MILLIONAIRE WITH PLENTY TO HIDE.

The argument

Getting the picture

Study the Deighton Developments press release. It has five paragraphs.

1. Which paragraph contains most of the facts about the business park?
2. Which paragraph contains most of the facts about housing?
3. Which paragraph(s) are mainly intended to **persuade** the reader?

Study the RAGE press release. It has four paragraphs.

4. Which paragraph(s) contain(s) most factual information?
5. Which paragraph tells you about the organisation RAGE?
6. Which paragraph tells you what RAGE plans to do?

◆ **Deighton** ◆
Developments

PRESS RELEASE

RIVERSIDE BUSINESS PARK

AN EXCITING NEW BUSINESS OPPORTUNITY!
A NEW DEAL FOR WYEDEAN!

Deighton Developments announce a bold and exciting new plan for the West of England. In association with its sister company Deighton Investments, the Company plans to develop a 100-acre site on the edge of Wyedean village, Hereford & Worcester.

Just over half the site, an area of 62 acres, will be developed as a high technology park, consisting of units varying in size from 500 square feet to 10,000 square feet. We aim to give scope for a wide range of businesses in the electronics, information technology, and aerospace fields. It is anticipated that the business park will create employment for about 300/400 highly skilled workers, with another 200+ jobs in the semi-skilled and service areas. There is high unemployment in this area, so the development will make a real contribution to the economy of the region.

The remaining 38 acres will be used for housing. It is planned to build a mix of different house types, from 5-bedroom executive homes, to 2-bedroom starter homes. Many houses will have either a river frontage, or direct access to the river bank. Fishing rights will be available to all house purchasers. The total number of houses to be built will be 362, offering accommodation to approximately 1100 people, in an area where housing of any kind is at a premium.

Detailed planning applications have now been lodged with the local authority and it is expected that there will be a public enquiry into the scheme, with all interested parties represented.

This part of England is in industrial decline. Riverside Business Park offers opportunities and a way forward. Forward to growth, prosperity and a confident future.

The language of persuasion

Each press release uses words that make its argument sound strong.

7   Read the Deighton Development press release. Find at least four words that have been chosen for their effect and explain what you think their effect is on the reader.

8   Now do the same with the RAGE press release.

Writing a comparison

Now write a paragraph comparing the two press releases. Comment on:

1   the information each gives;
2   the language used in each;
3   how effective each one is in persuading the reader to agree with the line it takes.

Radical Action for a Green Environment

PRESS RELEASE

RIVERSIDE VANDALISM!

Deighton Developments, a London-based property company, is planning to desecrate one of the most beautiful areas of the Wye Valley. In the name of progress - by which they mean maximum profit for them - they plan to dig up 100 acres of beautiful water meadows along the banks of the River Wye, and turn them into an industrial wasteland.
The fields, known locally as Grummer's Meadows, after the family who have farmed them for centuries, are a prized location for naturalists. They offer a unique habitat for a wide range of plants, flowers, insects and butterflies. The Chairperson of the Hereford and Radnor Nature Trust has said that their destruction would be an ecological catastrophe. Deighton Developments Chairperson Barry Deighton acknowledges this. He says that you can't make an omelette without cracking eggs, but 'People come first and this scheme will make jobs for people.' How shortsighted can you get?
Local groups are already protesting vigorously, in the run-up to the public enquiry due to open shortly. RAGE intends to make its presence felt, both before and during the enquiry.
Formed only three years ago, RAGE has already successfully opposed a number of similar development schemes, including a marina at Holtby on the Norfolk Broads, and a riverside 'Technivillage' on the Hampshire Avon. RAGE intends to make the Riverside Business Park another scalp to add to the list.

Public enquiry

What is a public enquiry?

A public enquiry is set up by the Department of the Environment to investigate an important planning issue. An **Inspector** is appointed and told to *find out the facts* and to *decide on the strength of the arguments* for and against. S/he then makes a **recommendation** saying whether or not the development should go ahead.

An enquiry is **not** a debate or a discussion. What happens is that the Inspector asks experts to advise him or her and invites people with a serious point of view to present their arguments and evidence. They state their case and may then be questioned by the Inspector and his advisers. They may also be questioned by a representative of any group that disagrees with them. Even then it is more like a trial than a debate.

THE ENQUIRY

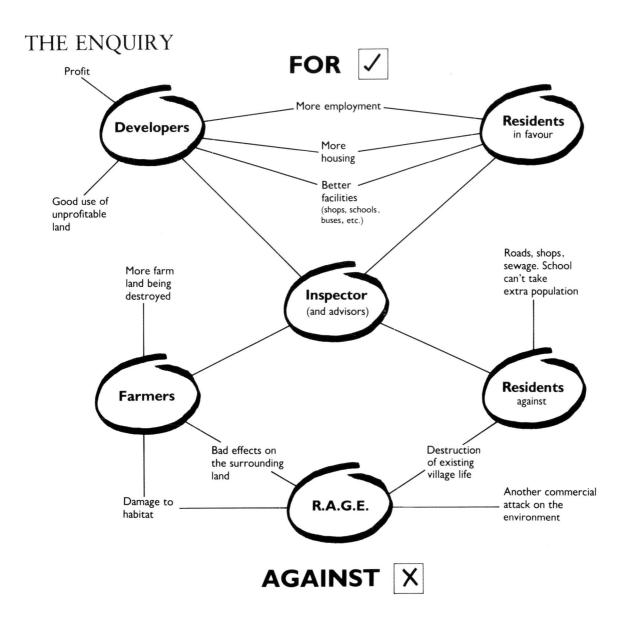

FOR ☑

Profit

Developers

Good use of
unprofitable
land

More employment

More
housing

Better
facilities
(shops, schools,
buses, etc.)

Residents
in favour

More farm
land being
destroyed

Inspector
(and advisors)

Roads, shops,
sewage. School
can't take
extra population

Farmers

Residents
against

Bad effects on
the surrounding
land

Destruction
of existing
village life

Damage to
habitat

R.A.G.E.

Another commercial
attack on the
environment

AGAINST X

Group work: preparing a case

Your group represents one of the five groups
at the public enquiry. You have to prepare
your case for presentation to the Inspector.

1   Talk together and prepare a detailed case
    for your group.
2   All make notes on the arguments you
    decide to put forward.
3   Decide how you will present the case.
    Divide the presentation up so that each
    person in the group takes part.
4   Practise the presentation so that it is
    clear, fluent, and confident.

Writing: developing a case

Imagine that you have been chosen as the
main speaker for your group. You have to
make the introductory speech presenting your
case to the Enquiry. Use the notes you have
made and the ideas you have discussed, and
write the text of your speech.

Developments

Following the story up

How does the public enquiry end? What happens next? Write a conclusion to the story in one of the following forms:

  as a magazine or newspaper article
  as part of the diary of one of the people involved
  as a local radio or TV broadcast

Use your own ideas, or continue one of these:

to hear that the development plan had been rejected and we had won!! I couldn't believe my ears when it was announced. In fact at first I thought there must have been some mistake. But then Bridget came across the hall with a smile all over her face...

Presenter: . . . that the plan to build a high-tech Business Park in the lovely village of Wyedean has been given the go-ahead. With me in the studio, I have a representative of Deighton Developments, Anne Marlowe.
Marlowe: Good evening.
Presenter: And a leading opponent of the plan, environmentalist Alison Graham of RAGE, the pressure group whose initials stand for Radical Action for a Green Environment.
Graham: Hello.
Presenter: Anne Marlowe, let me turn to you first. What does this decision mean for the village of Wyedean?

Self-assessment

Look at the list of **English activities** on page 65. Use it as a guide to remind you of what you have covered. Write a brief assessment of your work on this unit:

● what you did
● what you found easy or difficult
● what you found interesting or boring
● what you think you did well
● areas where you need more practice
● what you think you learned from the unit
● your overall impression of the work

Work experience

This unit takes you through the stages of work experience. It gives you an idea of what is involved and provides practice in the different kinds of language involved.

English activities

In this unit, you will get the chance to think, talk, and write about work experience. If you have already done work experience, you will have a chance to think about what you did and share your experiences with other people. If you have not, then it will give you a taste of what work experience is like and what its purpose is. You will undertake these English activities:

> discussion
>> in pairs
>> in small groups
> role-play: an interview
> reading and understanding non-literary material
> writing
>> a formal letter
>> personal response
>> expressing opinion

Applying

Factory Hands and Machine Operators required.
Clean work, reasonable Pay and Conditions.
Write in the first instance to:

Mr. C. Sedge,
Firmaweld Ltd.,
Halter Road,
Westfield Industrial Estate,
Marketon.
Yo11 3UP

ELIZABETH COURT RESTAURANT

18/20 The Crescent,
Lowtown,
North Yorkshire. YO21 8BA
Telephone: Scarborough (0891) 5678

KITCHEN ASSISTANT REQUIRED

APPLICANT MUST BE INTERESTED IN DEALING WITH
ALL ASPECTS OF CATERING.

FULL BASIC TRAINING GIVEN WITH OPPORTUNITY
TO BECOME FULLY QUALIFIED COOK OR CHEF

PLEASE APPLY MISS BARNARD AT ABOVE ADDRESS.

NIXON'S
TV & ELECTRICAL

OFFICE JUNIOR AGE 16/17
REQUIRED FOR GENERAL TYPING
AND OFFICE DUTIES
MUST BE OF SMART APPEARANCE
WITH GOOD TELEPHONE MANNER
APPLY IN WRITING TO:

Mr. S. J. MASON
Nixon's,
7 & 9 East Avenue,
Mile End,
NW1 4PJ

TRAINEE FARM SECRETARY

**A young person is required to work in the Offices of an
Agricultural Consultancy to train as a Farm Secretary.** Initial
duties will be filing and telephone operator, but training will
be given in Farm Secretarial work, with a view to becoming a
travelling Farm Secretary.

The successful Applicant will be expected to become, if not
already, a competent Shorthand Typist, if necessary by Night
School study. Opportunity will be given to learn to drive.

Apply in own handwriting, with references to:

Mr. D. Harwood,
East Midshire Farm Services,
16, Queen Street,
Middleton.

Oasis Holidays
AN OASIS LEISURE COMPANY

Windy Bay Holiday Park
Windy Bay, Filey, Norfolk. NO2 5PJ Telephone: 0910 421789

GENERAL HANDYPERSON
REQUIRED

To work in our Maintenance Department.
Training given in basic Joinery, Plumbing, Painting and Electrics.
Some basic knowledge of one of the above would be an advantage.
Apply in writing to: Mr. P. Best, Maintenance Manager, at the above address.

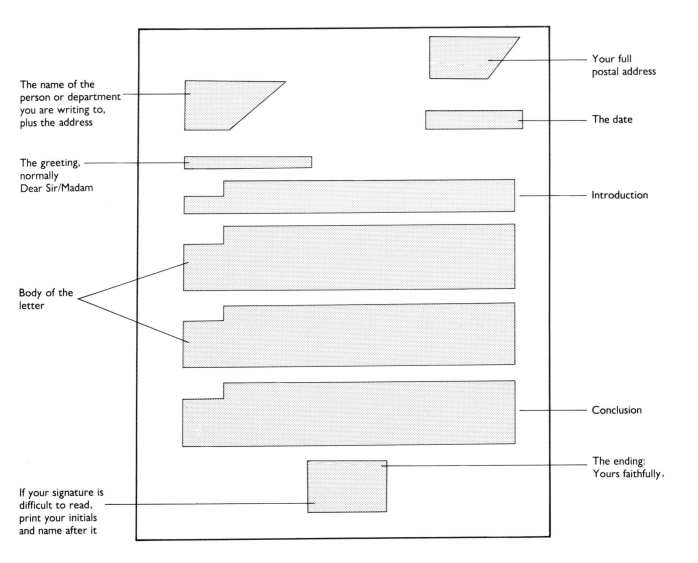

The name of the person or department you are writing to, plus the address

Your full postal address

The greeting, normally Dear Sir/Madam

The date

Introduction

Body of the letter

Conclusion

The ending: Yours faithfully,

If your signature is difficult to read, print your initials and name after it

What to do

You are going to apply for one of these jobs as your work experience. Choose carefully which job will suit you best, bearing in mind the type of work you wish to do when you leave school. It is unlikely that the jobs advertised here will fit your own requirements exactly, but one or more of them may demand the same sort of skills which will be needed for your own chosen career.

1 Choose the advert you are going to reply to.
2 Think carefully what you want to say to the employer.
3 Write a rough version of the **body** of the letter.
4 Write a rough version of the **introduction** and **conclusion**.
5 Read it all through and alter it until you are satisfied with it.
6 Now write the final version, setting it out correctly.
7 Check it carefully.

Pair work option

While you can do this exercise on your own, you may find it helpful to work with a partner. In real life you will often find that when you have to write a letter like this, it is easier if you can consult someone whose opinion you trust.

The interview

Preparation

For this exercise, work with a partner.

1   Decide who will be the **interviewer** and who will be the **applicant**.
2   The applicant should give the interviewer **his/her** letter of application.
3   The interviewer should also look at the advert which the applicant was responding to.
4   Now study your separate instructions on this page.

Interviewer

1   Study the advert and make sure that you can answer these questions.
    What kind of work does this firm do?
    What kind of work are we offering this applicant?
    What special qualities or skills will s/he need?
    What is my job?
2   Read the applicant's letter and make **brief** notes on these points.
    What is my first impression of this applicant's:
        personality
        neatness and efficiency
        willingness to work
        special qualities.

    What do I want to ask him/her?

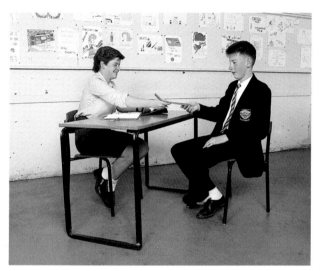
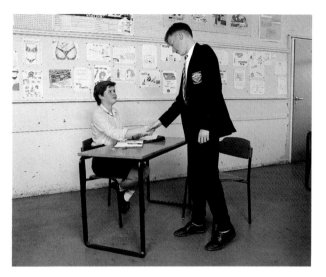

Applicant

Work out the answers to these questions:

1. What do I need to find out about the business?
2. What do I need to find out about the kind of work involved?
3. What have I to offer this job?
4. What new skills will I need?
5. What questions do I want to ask at the interview?
6. How should I dress for the interview?
7. What do I need to remember at the interview about:
   a) how to speak
   b) how to behave.

The interview

Arrange your two chairs so that you can sit facing each other. When you are ready, begin with the applicant coming into the interview room.

After the interview

1. Both make notes on what happened:
   Interviewer your impressions of the applicant, how suitable s/he would be, and why.
   Applicant your impressions of the firm; whether you would like to work there; how well you did.
2. Discuss the interview and the notes you have just made.

Contact

Work Experience Scheme 19

Name of Organisation: _____

Pupil on work experience: _____

<u>Basic information</u>

Hours of work (Pupils to work the hours of a normal employee):

_____

Lunch arrangements (If applicable please include the cost of a canteen meal):

_____

Clothing requirements (Clothing provided?):

_____

Where to report on the first day, and to whom:

_____

Any other useful information (transport provision, etc.):

_____

<u>Other points</u>

The pupil can be released for a half-day to finalise details with you, in the week before work experience begins.

If such a meeting is necessary, please state the day and time most suitable for you:

_____

It is hoped that a member of the school staff will be able to visit the pupil at some time during work experience, and speak to the person responsible for overseeing the pupil.

Name of person to be contacted: _____

Signed _____

Position _____

What to do

Discussion

What will be the main differences between a day of work experience and a day of school?

- before work (getting up, dressing, getting there)
- at work (what you do, people, interest)
- breaks (number, length, food and drink)
- after work (getting home, tiredness, etc.)

Writing

What I expect work experience to be like
Mention lots of things that occur to you, or concentrate on one or two. Make sure that your writing shows thought, and is organised sensibly.

First day

Work experience Log Book

Pupil: Ashley Harris
Place of Work: Rodgers cafe
Type of Work: General assistant

Day 1

What a start! 10 minutes late because my bike had a puncture. The way Mr Rodgers went on, you'd think it was my fault. I spent the first part of the morning washing the floors, and then I was promoted to washing windows. Big deal! Mr Rodgers set me on defrosting the fridges, one at a time, but that didn't last long because he came roaring in, shouting that I'd have to do the windows again because they were worse than when I'd started. What does he expect? I'm not going to keep trotting backwards and forwards for clean water – the kitchen's miles away!

I thought I'd have my lunchbreak at twelve, but just before then I had to clear tables, wipe them down and re-set them for the next customers. Talk about slave labour! I never stopped until half past one when it quietened down a bit, I went to take my overall off to go home, but Mr Rodgers nearly blew a fuse and told me to give a hand with the washing-up. I didn't get a break until nearly three o'clock.

When I got back I stayed out of his way. I kept looking busy, so he didn't bother me at all. Sue – she's in charge of the waitresses, sort of – let me wait on at a couple of tables when it was fairly quiet. I was doing all right, but the customers kept complaining. I was glad when 6 o'clock came round. I said 'Goodnight' to Mr Rodgers, but he gave me a funny look and said 'I'll speak to you tomorrow.' Could it be promotion already?

Questions to think about

1 What do you think of the work Ashley Harris is being asked to do?
2 What does this extract tell us about Mr Rodgers?
3 What does this extract tell us about Ashley Harris?

Writing

In **script** form you are going to write an account of their meeting the next day.
You might begin:
Mr Rodgers: Sit down. (Pause) Now, look, I'm seriously considering ringing the school...

Reactions

Boy: I was welcomed by everyone and helped by everyone when I got into difficulty.

Girl: In the second week the part-time worker was not there so I was relied on to do her work. I enjoyed the responsibility.

Father: Since his work experience he has been a lot more pleasant at home.

Father: She learned that work means being part of a team, and this has helped her to mature a little, I feel.

Mother: He told us in detail what he had done each day. A big advantage was that he was so tired he went to bed early!

Café owner: A bit slow on the uptake, but very willing – that's what matters.

Butcher: A most pleasant young man. He did everything that was asked for. He began with a shy approach but with more time with us we would really sort that out. He just needs someone to take an interest in him.

Discussion

Read all the comments carefully. Then consider and discuss your answers to these questions about each one:

1   What does it tell us about the boy or girl on work experience?
2   What does it tell us about the employer?
3   What does it tell us about any other person(s) mentioned?
4   Has this piece of work experience been worthwhile?

Writing

Under the heading **Work Experience**, write three paragraphs with these subheadings:

Advantages to the pupil
The parent's view
The role of the employer

Use the comments on this page to help you, but add material and ideas of your own.

Evaluation

Work Experience: Pupil Evaluation Sheet

1. Name...

2. Place of work...

3. Type of work allocated to:...............................
   Was this what you wanted to try?........................

4. Approximate total cost during the ten days of a) transport..........
   b) meals.............

5. Your views on the work (put a line through those statements that are not true).

   a) Liked it most of the time/some of the time/little of the time/not at all.

   b) Found it easy most of the time/some of the time/little of the time/not at all.

   c) Found it tiring most of the time/some of the time/little of the time/not at all.

   d) Found it interesting most of the time/some of the time/little of the time/not at all.

   e) It was what you thought it would be like most of the time/some of the time/little of the time/not at all.

   f) Workers were friendly towards you most of the time/some of the time/little of the time/not at all.

   g) It had plenty of variety/some variety/not very much/none.

   h) You learned a lot/a little/not very much/nothing.

6. Remembering the two aims of the scheme (a) to give you experience of the discipline of going to work and (b) to give you experience of a particular type of work how would you rate your experience in achieving:

   Aim (a) thoroughly successful/quite successful/not very successful/unsuccessful.

   (b) thoroughly successful/quite successful/not very successful/unsuccessful.

   Comments:

7. On the back of this form list ten activities that you carried out.

8. Which of these did you enjoy most?...........................

9. Has your experience: encouraged you to try and enter this kind of work/put you off this kind of work/left you still unsure?

10. Has there been any positive outcome to your period of work experience? (e.g. offer of a job, decision to continue in full time education, etc.)..

11. Did you have any particular problems during your period of work experience?..

12. Have you any suggestions as to how the scheme could be improved on future occasions?...

Here is a form to be completed by pupils at the end of their work experience. The purpose of the form is to help school staff:

a) find out each pupil's reaction to the scheme;

b) improve the scheme for future years.

You might find this form complicated in some parts, irrelevant in others. For instance, could the information which comes out of Question 5 be expressed in a simpler way? Does the information required in Question 7 really matter?

Look carefully at the form.

1 Write a criticism of the form. Say which parts of the form could be improved, and how you would improve them. Include comment on those parts of the form which you think are good, giving your reasons for your opinion.

2 Write out your own pupil evaluation sheet, using a layout similar to the one above.

Developments

1 Ashley Harris (page 81, this unit) has completed his work experience.
   Write: a) the comments of Ashley
          b) the comments of Mr Harris
          c) the comments of Mr Rodgers
   In Ashley's last term at school he applies for a job, and the prospective employer asks the Head for a reference.
   Write: d) the part of the Head's report on Ashley which refers to his work experience.
2 How realistic do you think work experience is? Write two or three paragraphs on the differences between work experience and 'the real thing'.

If you have been on a work experience scheme:

3 Write of your own experience. Mention your expectations and the reality. What was the value to you, and your employer, in terms of working with other people, experience of the job, responsibility and attitude?
4 Write a letter of thanks to your employer. In this situation a mere thank you is not enough! Now that you know the person concerned you begin the letter Dear Mr . . . . . . or Dear Mrs/Miss/Ms . . . . . and you end Yours sincerely.

English assessment

The work you have done on this unit can contribute to your assessment in the following ways:

Role-play and discussions can form part of your spoken English assessment.
The letters are practice in writing in 'closed' situations/directed writing either for an exam, or for a coursework folder.
Writing about your own response or experience can go into your coursework folder.
Working through the unit gives good practice in reading and understanding non-literary material.

Self-assessment

Look at the list of **English activities** on page 75. Use it as a guide to remind you of what you have covered. Write a brief assessment of your work on this unit:

- what you did
- what you found easy or difficult
- what you found interesting or boring
- what you think you did well
- areas where you need more practice
- what you think you learned from the unit
- your overall impression of the work

Volunteer

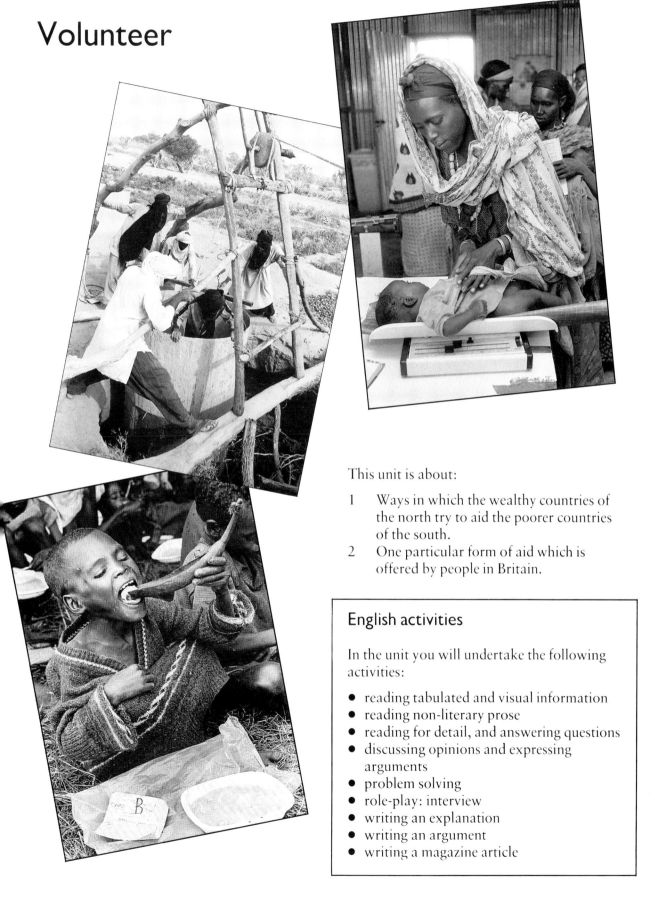

This unit is about:

1   Ways in which the wealthy countries of
    the north try to aid the poorer countries
    of the south.
2   One particular form of aid which is
    offered by people in Britain.

English activities

In the unit you will undertake the following
activities:

- reading tabulated and visual information
- reading non-literary prose
- reading for detail, and answering questions
- discussing opinions and expressing
  arguments
- problem solving
- role-play: interview
- writing an explanation
- writing an argument
- writing a magazine article

How can we help?

These are some of the ways in which people in countries of the north have helped the countries of the Third World.

Disaster relief

EXAMPLES   Ethiopia
Mozambique

ARGUMENTS
FOR
Arouses public concern
Raises a lot of money
Gets help where it is needed

AGAINST
Often comes far too late
Never gets down to the real problem
Doesn't help people to avoid future disasters
It's just a way for people to salve their consciences

Government grants and loans

EXAMPLES
Grants of money or loans for -
Purchase of agricultural equipment
Development of industries and purchase of equipment
Improvement of communications: roads, railways, etc

ARGUMENTS
FOR
More carefully planned: can get help where needed
Long-term - spread over a number of years
Helps to develop the country's economy

AGAINST
Depends on politicians: if the government changes...
Can turn into blackmail: do as we say or...
Governments often expect something in return - trade, military bases...

Technical assistance

EXAMPLES

Sending qualified people to work in:
Education
Engineering
Agriculture

ARGUMENTS FOR

Helps to train new teachers, engineers and farmers
Has long-term effects
Good value for money
Increases understanding between countries

AGAINST

Takes a long time to have any effect
Human factor - projects may go wrong
Still quite expensive

What to do

Solo work

Study the material on these two pages. Make sure that you understand:

a) what each kind of aid involves
b) the meaning of the arguments for
c) the meaning of the arguments against

Discussion

1 Why should people in a country like Britain give any aid at all to Third World countries?
2 Almost every year there is a famine or similar disaster somewhere in the world. Often thousands, even millions, of people are at risk. Would it be a good idea to say, 'All the money this country has for aid will be saved for famine and disaster relief'?
3 Which is a better way to use money: government grants or technical assistance? What are your reasons?

How can I help?

A I remember watching Top of the Pops and the Band Aid record a couple of years ago and the video that went with it. I think that that was really the first time that people in this country had really been forced to sit up and take notice whether they wanted to or not . . . my reaction was sell the cottage, get straight out there and do something . . . and they said, 'Well there's no point – you're not trained in anything: there's nothing you can do. You'll get out there, you'll be sick yourself. You won't be able to help anybody else. You'll have to be flown home. You're just another mouth to feed.' It was a feeling of almost helplessness to feel that there was desperately something that had to be done but not really being able to do anything practical to help . . .

B The only time that I thought of overseas is like in Saudi Arabia or something like that because that's where all the big money is. Years ago I had ideas of being this amazing plant mechanic in the Middle East earning £50,000–60,000 a year tax-paid. I'd never really thought about doing charity work until Live Aid actually. So when Live Aid came around and I heard about the transport problem with the trucks breaking down it seemed like a good opportunity – I've never been so sure about something in my life . . . that's the sort of thing I want to do – they just need your skills – somebody actually wants you. So I wrote to them . . . I got a letter back on behalf of Bob Geldof saying 'Thank you, but no, thank you' sort of thing. So I thought 'All right, what else can I do?' Somebody said 'Well why don't you do VSO?' I said 'What's that?' They showed me a little coupon in *The Guardian*. I said 'What's it about?'

adapted from *Fears, Fantasies and Expectations* (BBC/VSO tape)

Read the two extracts and then answer these questions:

1 What made both speakers want to do something to help?
2 Did either of them have any idea of how to help? If so, what?
3 Why were they both rejected?
4 What opinion did you form of each person, and why?

VSO

What to do

Read the advert and answer these questions:

1. a) What kind of help does VSO think is most needed in the Third World?
   b) What do they mean by the heading 'Technical'?
   c) How does VSO prepare volunteers for work overseas?
   d) How long are the volunteers expected to work abroad?
   e) How much are they paid?

2. Speaker B said about VSO, 'What's it about?' Use the information in the advert to help you write a brief explanation for him.

Which project?

Every year VSO studies many different projects for which it could recruit volunteers. Its funds are limited, so it has to choose which projects are the most suitable. On these two pages are details of some possible projects.

Philippines

The project

St Mark's technical school was set up five years ago as a joint venture between the local Roman Catholic mission and VSO. The mission already ran a secondary school, but did not have the staff or experience to run a technical school. VSO sent Graham Frewin, a mechanical engineer, who set up the school and became its first Principal.

Students were aged between 15 and 50 years, and were mainly local tradesmen or young unemployed people, living in squatter settlements. When Frewin left, there were over 500 students and 19 Filipino instructors. His Filipino Deputy Principal was ready to take over. VSO have now been asked to send a second volunteer to teach toolmaking. This would extend the range of skills being taught at the school.

The Gambia

The project

The Gambia is a small country, with few qualified lawyers. The government has started a law reform programme. Their present laws are still based on those of Britain. Now they want to change some of them, to include local traditions and customs. These changes will have an important effect on family life and the rights of women. The Government has asked for a volunteer with suitable experience to help with the research.

Kenya

The project

Kenya is a very poor country with an expanding population. Farming cannot employ very many people, because the amount of suitable land is limited. So the unemployed move into the towns, but then find that there is nowhere to live and no work to do.

In a village near Thika a co-operative has been formed to improve the local environment. They have a 28,000 acre estate, and some government money to provide materials. Part of the project involves building new housing to encourage people to stay in the area and farm the land. There are plenty of people willing to work. Some of these have basic building skills. They need someone to help them design model houses that members of the co-operative can copy. They also need help with organising the scheme.

(All these projects are based on work actually undertaken by VSO and described in its *Annual Review* for 1987.)

What to do

1 Read the descriptions and look at the pictures.
2 Imagine that you have to recommend just **one** of the projects to VSO. Decide which you would choose.
3 Make a list of reasons for choosing your project.
4 Write a brief explanation of your choice.

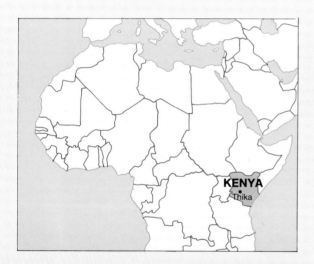

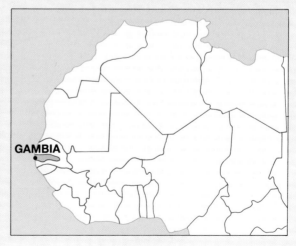

Selection

The project

Kitua is a district in southern Tanzania. It is a farming area, but the people are poor and there are serious health problems caused by a variety of communicable diseases. There is a mobile Health Clinic, which serves a wide area, but its work has been held up by lack of funds and lack of qualified nurses. VSO has been asked to recruit a nurse who will lead one of the health teams going round providing health care and educating the local people about how to avoid common diseases. In addition, the nurse chosen will be expected to train her/his successor, so that after two years, when the volunteer returns to Britain, a Tanzanian can take over. The following letter has been received from the VSO Field Officer in Tanzania.

... so that conditions there are not easy. It is a very remote area, with few opportunities to get into a town or do any shopping. Whoever is recruited will have to be very self-reliant. He/she will have to live largely on the local diet (mainly vegetarian) and share a small house with the Tanzanian nurse he/she will be working with. Mains electricity and pumped water are available, but both often break down. It gets very hot and dusty – not a healthy climate!

Also there are a number of other problems. The leader of the Health team has recently had a row with the District Council and there is what amounts to a feud between them – members of the council keep trying to interfere with the running of the clinic. In one case this even led to physical violence. The volunteer chosen will have to be both determined and tactful. She or he will also need to have a very stable personality and background, and be able to cope with frequent setbacks.

The applicants

What to do

On these two pages are details of three people who have applied to do VSO. They are being considered for the post at Kitua. All have the necessary qualifications. Study the information about each one. It consists of:

> photograph
> brief personal details
> part of a reference written by someone who knows the person well
> part of the person's letter of application

When you have read it and thought about it, decide who you would recommend for the posting and why.

Lois McIntyre

Age: 23   Single

She has the minimum experience required

Interests: Athletics, mountaineering ski-ing, karate

REFERENCE

She is a lively, energetic and cheerful person who works - and plays - hard. She is very popular in the hospital, being a friendly and sociable person. I believe that she now feels free to apply for VSO, because her mother, whom she looked after devotedly, has now passed away. I have no hesitation in recommending her.

Now that I have no responsibilities to tie me down, I feel that I should like to travel and see the world. I also feel that because I have been lucky in life, I should like to help those who are less fortunate than myself. VSO seems to me an ideal way of combining these two aims.

For some years I have wanted the opportunity to work in a Third World country. I believe that I have skills and experience that I can share with others. Until recently this has not been possible. Now that I am divorced, I have the opportunity to fulfil this ambition. It will also give me a chance to get away from immediate worries and see my life in perspective.

REFERENCE

Michael Johnson is an experienced and committed nurse. He is a bit of a loner, but this is by choice rather than because he doesn't get on with people. In fact he can be a loyal and a reliable friend, as those who know him well will agree. I recommend him very strongly for VSO, because he has a strong belief in helping others - although I know that he will be very sadly missed if he leaves our hospital.

REFERENCE

Anne Barstowe is a most experienced and highly qualified nurse. She has worked in a number of hospitals and in a variety of different types of ward. She is hardworking and very determined. She applies the highest standards to herself and to those with whom she works. Sometimes her determination may make her apparently tactless or 'difficult', but this is usually because she wants to provide the best possible care for patients.

Now that I have had a lot of training and experience in different hospitals, I want to share this with people in countries that are less well off than Britain. I should like to do this while I am still young enough and fit enough to be able to do it properly, because I cannot stand jobs that are not done as well as they can be!

Developments

Writing

As you have worked through this unit, you have learned about the aims and work of VSO. Use this information for one of the following writing assignments:

1   A short article about VSO for a teenage magazine. (You could include made-up quotations from volunteers in different parts of the world.)
2   An account of how someone volunteered and was eventually selected. (You could begin with one of the two people quoted on page 88.)

Role-play: interviews

Solo preparation

You are going to be interviewed as one of the applicants on pages 93-4.

1   Read the two pages again and choose which person to be.
2   Study *your* details carefully. Make up any extra information you think you may need.
3   Think about the person. In particular, make sure that you know *why* s/he has decided to apply for VSO.

You will also have to be an interviewer.

4   Make a list of questions to help you to find out about the applicant's experience, personality, and interests.

Pair work: the interview

5   Decide who will be the candidate first.
6   Carry out the interview.
7   When you have finished, discuss how it went. In particular try to decide – **honestly** – whether the candidate came across as a suitable person for the job.
8   Now swap over.

English assessment

The work you have done on this unit can contribute to your assessment in the following ways:

Role-play and discussions can form part of your spoken English assessment.
The magazine article is practice in writing in 'closed' situations/directed writing either for an exam, or for a coursework folder.
Writing about your own opinions can go into your coursework folder.
Working through the unit gives good practice in reading and understanding non-literary material.

Self-assessment

Look at the list of **English activities** on page 85. Use it as a guide to remind you of what you have covered. Write a brief assessment of your work on this unit:

● what you did
● what you found easy or difficult
● what you found interesting or boring
● what you think you did well
● areas where you need more practice
● what you think you learned from the unit
● your overall impression of the work

What kind of world?

Geography lesson

When the jet sprang into the sky,
it was clear why the city
had developed the way it had,
seeing it scaled six inches to the mile.
There seemed an inevitability
about what on ground had looked haphazard,
unplanned and without style
when the jet sprang into the sky.

When the jet reached ten thousand feet,
it was clear why the country
had cities where rivers ran
and why the valleys were populated.
The logic of geography –
that land and water attracted man –
was clearly delineated
when the jet reached ten thousand feet.

When the jet rose six miles high,
it was clear that the earth was round
and that it had more sea than land.
But it was difficult to understand
that the men on the earth found
causes to hate each other, to build
walls across cities and to kill.
From that height, it was not clear why.

Zulfikar Ghose

The watchman

There was still a faint splash of red on the western horizon. The watchman
stood on the tank bund and took a final survey. All the people who had come
for evening walks had returned to their homes. Not a soul anywhere – except
that obstinate angler, at the northern end, who sat with his feet in water,
sadly gazing on his rod. It was no use bothering about him: he would sit
there till midnight, hoping for a catch.

   The Taluk office gong struck nine. The watchman was satisfied that no
trespassing cattle had sneaked in through the wire fencing. As he turned to
go, he saw, about a hundred yards away, a shadowy figure moving down the
narrow stone steps that led to the water's edge. He thought for a second that
it might be a ghost. He dismissed the idea, and went up to investigate. If it
was anyone come to bathe at this hour . . . From the top step he observed that
it was a woman's form. She stooped over the last step and placed something
on it – possibly a letter. She then stepped into knee-deep water, and stood
there, her hands pressed together in prayer. Unmistakable signs – always to
be followed by the police and gruesome details, bringing the very worst
possible reputation to a tank.

   He shouted, 'Come out, there, come out of it.' The form looked up from
the water. 'Don't stand there and gaze. You'll catch a cold, come up whoever
you are . . . .' He raced down the steps and picked up the letter. He hurriedly
lit his lamp, and turned its wick till it burnt brightly, and held it up,
murmuring: 'I don't like this. Why is everyone coming to the same tank? If
you want to be dead, throw yourself under an engine,' he said.

98

The light fell upon the other's face. It was a young girl's, wet with tears. He felt a sudden pity. He said, 'Sit down, sit down and rest . . . no, no . . . go up two more steps and sit down. Don't sit so near the water . . . .' She obeyed. He sat down on the last step between her and the water, placed the lantern on the step, took out a piece of tobacco, and put it in his mouth. She buried her face in her hands, and began to sob. He felt troubled and asked: 'Why don't you rise and go home, lady?'

She sputtered through her sob: 'I have no home in this world!'

'Don't tell me! Surely, you didn't grow up without a home all these years!' said the watchman.

'I lost my mother when I was five years old –' she said.

'I thought so . . .' replied the watchman, and added, 'and your father married again and you grew up under the care of your stepmother?'

'Yes, yes, how do you know?' she asked.

'I am sixty-five years old,' he said and asked, 'Did your stepmother trouble you?'

'No, there you are wrong,' the girl said. 'She is very kind to me. She has been looking after me ever since my father died a few years ago. She has just a little money on hand left by my father, and she spends it on us.'

The watchman looked at the stars, sighed for the dinner that he was missing. 'It's very late, madam, go home.'

'I tell you I've no home –' she retorted angrily.

'Your stepmother's house is all right from what you say. She is good to you.'

'But why should I be a burden to her? Who am I?'

'You are her husband's daughter,' the watchman said, and added, 'That is enough claim.'

'No no. I won't live on anybody's charity.'

'Then you will have to wait till they find you a husband –'

She glared at him in the dark. 'That's what I do not want to do. I want to study and become a doctor and earn my livelihood. I don't want to marry. I often catch my mother talking far into the night to her eldest son, worrying about my future, about my marriage. I know they cannot afford to keep me in college very long now; it costs about twenty rupees a month.'

'Twenty rupees!' the watchman exclaimed. It was his month's salary. 'How can anybody spend so much for books!'

'Till today,' she said, 'I was hoping that I would get a scholarship. That would have saved me. But this evening they announced; others have got it, not I. My name is not there –' and she broke down again. The watchman looked at her in surprise. He comprehended very little of all this situation. She added: 'And when they come to know of this, they will try to arrange my marriage. Someone is coming to have a look at me tomorrow.'

'Marry him and may God bless you with ten children.'

'No, no,' she cried hysterically. 'I don't want to marry. I want to study.'

The silent night was stabbed by her sobbing and some night bird rustled the water, and wavelets beat upon the shore. Seeing her suffer, he found his own sorrows in life came to his mind; how in those far-off times, in his little village home an epidemic of cholera laid out his father and mother and brothers on the same day, and he was the sole survivor; how he was turned out of his ancestral home through the trickery of his father's kinsmen, and he wandered as an orphan, suffering indescribable hunger and privation.

'Everyone has his own miseries,' he said. 'If people tried to kill themselves for each one of them, I don't know how often they would have to drown.' He remembered further incidents and his voice shook with sorrow. 'You are young and you don't know what sorrow is . . .' He remained silent and a sob broke out of him as he said: 'I prayed to all the gods in the world for a son. My wife bore me eight children. Only one daughter lives now, and none of the others saw the eleventh year . . .' The girl looked at him in bewilderment.

The Taluk office gong struck again. 'It is late, you had better get up and go home,' he said.

She replied: 'I have no home.'

He felt irritated. 'You are making too much of nothing. You should not be obstinate –'

'You don't know my trouble,' she said.

He picked up his lantern and staff and got up. He put her letter down where he found it.

'If you are going to be so obstinate, I'll leave you alone. No one can blame me.' He paused for a moment, looked at her, and went up the steps; not a word passed between them again.

The moment he came back to duty next morning, he hurried down the stone steps. The letter lay where he had dropped it on the previous night. He picked it up and gazed on it, helplessly, wishing that it could tell him about the fate of the girl after he had left her. He tore it up and flung it on the water. As he watched the bits float off on ripples, he blamed himself for leaving her and going away on the previous night. 'I am responsible for at least one suicide in this tank,' he often remarked to himself. He could never look at the blue expanse of water again with an easy mind. Even many months later he could not be certain that the remains of a body would not come up all of a sudden. 'Who knows, it sometimes happens that the body gets stuck deep down,' he reflected.

Years later, one evening as he stood on the bund and took a final survey before going home, he saw a car draw up on the road below. A man, a woman, and three children emerged from the car and climbed the bund. When they approached, the watchman felt a start at his heart; the figure and face of the woman seemed familiar to him. Though the woman was altered by years, and ornaments, and dress, he thought that he had now recognised the face he had once seen by the lantern light. He felt excited at this discovery. He had numerous questions to ask. He brought together his palms and saluted her respectfully. He expected she would stop and speak to him. But she merely threw at him an indifferent glance and passed on. He stood staring after her for a moment, baffled. 'Probably this is someone else,' he muttered and turned to go home, resolving to dismiss the whole episode from his mind.

R.K. Narayan

The new place

Welfare woman: May I come in then?

Man: Well, I . . .

Welfare woman: Just for a minute . . . Oh, well, now – aren't you lucky?

Man: Lucky?

Welfare woman: This lovely place. All clean and light.

Man: It's a bit pokey.

Welfare woman: Compact. Bedroom, kitchenette. All you want.

Man: I liked the old place.

Welfare woman: And the central heating. You can feel it as soon as you come into the building.

Man: Dries the air, though.

Welfare woman: What?

Man: I've always been used to a coal fire.

Welfare woman: A lot of trouble though. All that dirt. Your poor wife, she must have . . .

Man: I did all that. The fires. And the cleaning.

Welfare woman: Wonderful how you looked after her.

Man: There was no one else.

Welfare woman: But you mustn't think that. Not any more.

Man: Makes no difference really.

Welfare woman: You're bound to feel it. Bound to. After – how long was it – forty-two years?

(Silence)

Built-in cupboard too. We *are* posh.

(Silence)

Man: They never brought the piano.

Welfare woman: Piano?

Man: From Prince Albert Street.

Welfare woman: I think it was a question of room, really.

Man: Aye, there was plenty of room there. In the old place.

Welfare woman: *Too* big really. Those high ceilings.

Man: The old settee there. I didn't want that.

Welfare woman: Oh, it's a nice settee.

Man: What would I want with a settee? Here?

Welfare woman: We thought . . . you might like it. To put your feet up.

Man: I can go to bed when I want to put my feet up.

Welfare woman: Or, if you had friends in some time . . .

(Silence)

Did you play it, the piano?

Man: I used to, once. She . . . didn't like music.

Welfare woman: Well, I could mention it.

Man: It's a good one, German.

Welfare woman: I think Mr Brazendale said something about woodworm.

Man: It's old, that's why. It's a good one.

Welfare woman: I'll see about it.

Man: It could go over there. Instead of the couch.

Welfare woman: Yes... You don't think it would take the light away?
  (*Silence*)
Such a nice, big window. You can see right down the...double carriageway.
Man: I don't look out there much.
Welfare woman: I know how you must feel.

Man: What?
Welfare woman: But you mustn't cut yourself off just because...Look, if
  you find things getting you down, just tell someone.
Man: Who?
Welfare woman: Anyone. There's Mrs McQuade. She's promised to pop in
  every day.
Man: Mrs...?
Welfare woman: Just down the passage. Number 5A, I think.
Man: ·I don't know any Mrs McQuade...
Welfare woman: And there's the Welsh lady downstairs. Very active for her
  age. So you'll not be alone.
  (*Pause*)
Man: No.
Welfare woman: A bit of shopping, a library book to change...There'll
  always be someone...
  (*Silence*)
Well – I just thought I'd see how you'd settled in. You'll get to like it. You'll
  see...
  (*Silence*)
I'll pop in again. About Thursday, say. Goodbye...
  (*Door shuts*)
Man: I don't want any Mrs McQuade. I don't want any of them.
  (*Pause*)
Bloody settee. What would *I* want with a settee?

Len Rush

The shaft

Williamson looked up from the bunch of reports he was reading. Although he smiled around the lips, his eyes were worried.

'Sit down, Harry,' he said. 'Ah'll get through these first.' Harry sat down uneasily, rumpling his cap. Williamson went on with his pretence of reading the reports. There came another knock at the office door. Both men turned. Williamson put the reports carefully on to the desk. 'Come in!' he called out.

The man who entered could have been Harry's double. There was the same solid, medium build and sandy hair. Blue eyes set in a square face. A hard, uncompromising mouth. His eyes darted from Williamson to Harry, then back to Williamson. 'Morning, Mr Williamson,' he said. There was a strain of reproach mingling with the respect in his voice. 'Good morning, Willy,' Williamson said. 'Find a seat.' Willy found a seat, as far away from Harry as was possible.

Harry stood up. His lips were one thin bitter line. 'Ah dare-say our business can wait, Mr Williamson. Ah'll be at hand when ye want me.' He made for the door. Williamson sighed. This was going to be a tough job. 'You can sit down again, Harry. Ah want a word with both of ye.' He leaned back in his chair and tried to assume confidence.

'You'll both be wondering why Ah've asked you to call here today, eh?' Both men shifted uncomfortably. 'Well, it's awkward, dam' awkward, but it's got to stop, see? Seems everybody knew about this but me, or you'd have been on the carpet before now. What you do outside of work isn't any concern of mine, but when two men on a job like yours aren't on speaking terms, it's time to draw the line.' His eyes roved from the ceiling to the two silent men. Both stared back with rising hostility.

'What's the grumble?' asked Willy. 'We're keeping the shafts good; we do our work proper; so with all due respect to you, Mr Williamson, Ah think you're out of order.'

Williamson waved a placatory hand. 'No grumbles about your work; none, none at all. But this is what Ah'm getting at. You two don't speak? Right? Well, it's none of my business why, but remember you're on a responsible job. And accidents can happen in them shafts. Ah've seen one or two in my time. Accidents, mind ye. And what's people going to say if anything does happen to one of ye, eh?'

There was a long silence. 'We know our work,' said Harry at last. 'Nothing's going to happen.'

'It's between him and me,' said Willy. 'Personal; nothing to do with work, or with you.'

'That's right,' said Harry. 'It's our affair and ye needn't worry about it interfering with our work.'

Williamson thumped the table. 'My God!' he cried. 'Are ye men, or just bits of bairns? Can't ye see what Ah'm getting at? With the best will in the world anything can happen in a pit-shaft. . . .' As he spoke the words a sudden terrifying vision flashed across his mind. He saw two hundred fathoms of shaft vertically piercing the strata; a shadowy hole diminishing into extreme blackness. He saw the pipe-lined sides; pipes sucking unending gallons of water from underground dams; pipes carrying electric cables, and pipes through which rushed air, compressed to drive a thousand drills through virgin coal and naked rock. He saw the greasy black cables of the guides quiver like the key-cable of a web when a fly is enmeshed, and then a cage flash by with two figures on top, two men holding to the guy chains almost nonchalantly.

He switched his mind to the office; he had seen that picture a few times in the last few days; and always with a singularly sinister ending. Williamson possessed an imagination.

He raked both men with a significant glance. 'So it's got to stop! You can cut each other dead in the street, but by God, you'll speak at work! Either that, or one of you goes. That's final.' He fumbled with his reports. Both men remained seated, dumbly staring at him. 'That's all,' he said.

They walked out. Through his office window he saw them turn in opposite directions. A pity, he thought, two good workmen and brothers at that. Brothers! Well, they're not doing a Cain and Abel on this job. Give them a week, no more. Then one of them goes. Or both for that matter. That one or the other might capitulate never entered his mind. Williamson knew his men.

When Harry got home he found his wife busy with rolling-pin and dough, baking fadges and red with the fire's heat. A neat little woman with sharp features enclosed by a mop of hair which had earned for her the nickname of Ma Golliwog among the local bairns. 'Well?' she asked sharply. 'And what did Mr Williamson want with ye?'

He settled down gloomily in the big rocking-chair. 'Come to his ears about me an' Willy never speaking. Says it won't do.' She slammed the rolling-pin on to the table. 'Well, Ah'll be jiggered! A fine thing it is when the bosses start interfering with the men's family affairs. It won't do, eh? Well, it'll have to do, 'cos Ah'll nivver speak to that lot again! And Mr Williamson can like it or lump it.'

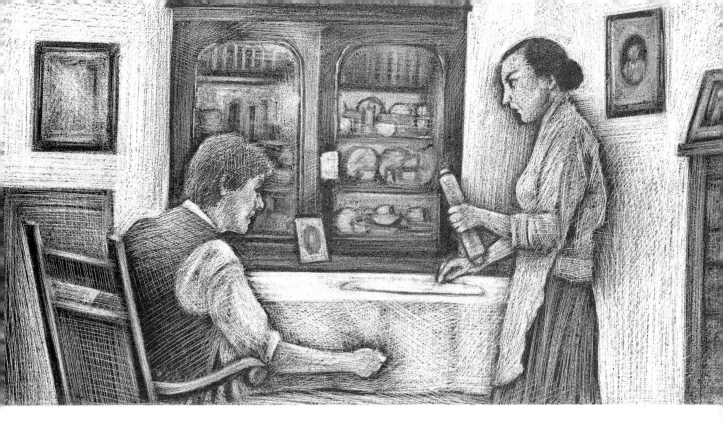

She picked up her rolling-pin and started to stamp, rather than roll, the unhappy dough. Then she looked up suspiciously. 'And what had you to say to him?'

'Told him it was our affair, and so did Willy.'

'Willy? Ye don't mean to tell me that he had ye both there? The impudence of the man!' she screeched, her eyes flashing fire.

'Said that if we don't settle the thing he's going to sack one of us.'

'Well, now, Harry Ward,' she said, quiet now, 'if you start speaking to that brother of yours, Ah'll leave you. So that's that.'

'Catch me speaking to him,' he said. 'Ah'll not forget him in a hurry.' But as he rocked the old chair he got to wondering how that slight seven stone of woman could hold so much bitterness. He sighed, then lit his pipe.

At the other side of the village much the same scene occurred at the home of Willy Ward. Willy may have been a little gloomier and his wife a trifle more bitter. After hearing the story, she repeated her determination not to patch up the quarrel, come what might. 'But what if Ah lose me job, honey?' said Willy. 'Might easily be me that has to go.'

'It'll not be you,' said his wife, confidently. 'You're twice as good a man as him. So you're not going to be first to break silence. Not after the way they carried on the day your Dad was buried. And all because he left them pictures to you. Not that they're very good pictures, they're not, and if it wasn't for the principle of the thing Ah'd let them have them. But there it is; the will was read, it was there in black and white for all the world to see! And then that screaming vulgar Lizzie had to start shoutin' at the top of her voice that they'd been promised to her. The very idea! No, it was them that started it and they shall finish it. D'ye hear what Ah say, Willy Ward?'

'Aye,' answered her husband, and went to bed for some sleep and peace. When he awoke the room was dark. A rattling window told of a high wind outside. He lay a moment, wishing he had another job and could lie in bed o' nights, instead of going out to work when others were going to sleep. Then he remembered the interview with Williamson and realised that his wish might soon come true. Groaning, he got out of bed and made his way downstairs. His supper was laid ready for him. 'Bit of a wind up,' he remarked. 'Aye, it's blown tiles off every roof in the street. And Mrs Roberts come in to say that the roof's been blown off the tin chapel!'

He had his supper and set off for work after another warning that there was to be no pact 'unless he speaks first'.

It *was* a wind! It billowed his raincoat out like a balloon and blew him, almost carried him, to the pit. Several times tiles and slates whizzed past his head to splinter into a thousand pieces at his feet. He was glad when he got to work. Harry was already in their cabin, changing into the warm, heavy clothes and buckling on his safety straps and belt. On a slate was chalked their work for that night. 'Loose guides in No. 1 shaft. Burst water-pipe in No. 2.' He glanced at the slate and proceeded to change.

It wasn't necessary to discuss which job should be done first. The burst pipe took precedence, since it would take longer to repair. Willy changed while Harry collected the gear needed. Not a word was said. When they went out the wind was blowing a gale. Harry was first out and he was swept back into the cabin like a ninepin, almost knocking Willy on to his back. There was no apology given, or expected.

They struggled against the wind until they reached 'the hole' at the base of the headstocks, then passed through an air-lock and entered the steel superstructure which covered the shaft. There they stood a moment, watching the cages sweep past with their cargoes of coal. Finally the electric bell above their heads shrilled six times. A door on the landing-level above them opened and the banksman appeared. 'All clear down there,' he shouted. Both men nodded. Used to their ways, he descended the spider-ladder to the duplicate controls.

'She's a raw, rough wind tonight,' he said. 'Aye she's rough,' said Harry. He tightened his safety-belt one hole. Worry had kept him from eating since the interview with Williamson. Davies rapped the cage to the level of the hole. It glided slowly into view, glistening wet with the sprayed water from the burst. The shaftmen stepped on the roof, fastened their safety-belts to the guy-chains, hung the gong, their only method of communication with Davies, then switched on their cap-lamps.

'Ready?' asked Davies. The wailing of the wind above, striking music from the pulley-wheels and girders, made him uneasy. There was something about the two men, also, that made for uneasiness, the way they walked without a flicker of an eyelid, or a motion of the hand. 'It's not natural,' he muttered. 'Brothers at that!' He watched intently, waiting for a nod from each. Each man took hold of the nearest guy-chain, then nodded.

He rapped away and watched the cage slowly sink into the black hole until it disappeared. Then, attaching the chain of the manual-signal to his hand, he walked to the edge of the shaft and peered down. He saw the two figures on the cage-top, curiously foreshortened in the glow of their lamps, like men viewed through the wrong end of a telescope. Indeed, the shaft itself, with its diminishing wet walls, was like the inside of a gigantic telescope. The gong sounded, its peal came echoing out of the depths, faint against the background of the gale that raged outside. He pulled the manual-chain urgently and sighed with relief as the greasy black steel ropes came to a standstill.

Down below, the cage was level with the burst pipe. A stream of water was sprayed from it, and the two men were soon soaked. They had a pair of clamps ready, but the pipe was out of reach when their safety-belts were attached, so they unfastened them, and proceeded to fix the clamps.

Harry had the inner clamp, and this meant he had to lie on the cage-top, holding his clamp in position with one hand while he held on to a guy-chain with the other, and Willy attached the other clamp and bolted it. It was an uncomfortable job for Harry, since the dripping water was ice-cold and his arm ached with the weight of the clamp.

And it was just at this moment that the gale above reached its peak, dislodging a rusting, insecure section of corrugated iron roofing. The wind lifted it as if it were no heavier than a sheet of newspaper, and pitched it unerringly into the narrow outlet of the superstructure. It swept past the astonished Davies and entered the shaft, ricocheting from side to side. The two men heard it coming. Harry pulled himself back on to his knees, letting the clamp drop. It crashed to the shaft-bottom, followed a split-second later by the section of roofing, which brushed, just brushed, Harry in passing.

But it was enough to knock him off his balance, and he would have followed clamp and roof-section had not Willy, by a purely reflex action, which was perfectly timed, caught him by the wrist. Harry's thirteen stone pulled Willy to the roof of the cage, but he still managed to hold on, with both hands clamped around one of Harry's wrists. He tried to pull his brother back, but found he was in no position for lifting; indeed, he imagined he heard his arms scrape in their sockets with the downward pull. Harry's dead-white face gazed up at him, running with sweat and water mixed. For the burst pipe was spraying directly above their heads. And, kick as hard as he could, Harry could not find even a bolt-head to support himself upon.

There was only one thing to do and that was to get the cage back to the level where Davies could help. But the gong was well out of reach. He locked one of his feet round a guy-chain and tried to kick out at the gong with the other. But it was too far away. There was only one thing left to do. He shouted. The Bull of Bashan had nothing on Willy that night. His desperate yell floated out of the blackness, and Davies, leaning over the shaft edge, heard it above the gale. '*Raise her to bank, Joe!*'

Davies pulled the manual chain and watched the sliding ropes, with his heart pounding. When the cage came into view he saw the situation immediately. He rapped hold and leaped on to grab the other arm. Even so, the two of them had a struggle to haul Harry back to safety. For a full five minutes all three lay on the cage top, panting for breath. Then Willy stood up. The other brother tried to follow suit but failed.

'Take it easy, now,' said Willy. Harry looked up. He had not heard that voice for months; he had not heard that particular note in it since they were lads together, the day he'd fallen in the river and lost a stocking, and Willy had met him going home, crying his eyes out. Then he smiled slowly. 'Always knew you'd be the one to break t'silence,' he said.

Willy had no immediate answer for this. His mind was on those few minutes of agony in the shaft. He had seen one man fall the full two hundred fathoms; he had seen the shattered, shapeless body wrapped in canvas. The Missus can play hell about me speaking first, he thought. Imagine Harry, me brother, lying down there, dead and broken. But he's alive, and Ah'd suffer a thousand nagging women for the joy of it.

'Mebbe Ah did break silence,' he said, 'but somebody had to speak, and since thou was so shook wi' fear, and Joe was out of breath a bit, it had to be me.'

Sid Chaplin

The flying machine

In the year AD 400, the Emperor Yuan held his throne by the Great Wall of China, and the land was green with rain, readying itself towards the harvest, at peace, the people in his dominion neither too happy nor too sad.

Early on the morning of the first day of the first week of the second month of the new year, the Emperor Yuan was sipping tea and fanning himself against a warm breeze when a servant ran across the scarlet and blue garden tiles, calling, 'Oh, Emperor, Emperor, a miracle!'

'Yes,' said the Emperor, 'the air *is* sweet this morning.'

'No, no, a miracle!' said the servant, bowing quickly.

'And this tea is good in my mouth, surely that is a miracle.'

'No, no, Your Excellency.'

'Let me guess then – the sun has risen and a new day is upon us. Or the sea is blue. *That* now is the finest of all miracles.'

'Excellency, a man is flying!'

'What?' The Emperor stopped his fan.

'I saw him in the air, a man flying with wings. I heard a voice call out of the sky, and when I looked up there he was, a dragon in the heavens with a man in its mouth, a dragon of paper and bamboo, coloured like the sun and the grass.'

'It is early,' said the Emperor, 'and you have just wakened from a dream.'

'It is early, but I have seen what I have seen! Come, and you will see it too.'

'Sit down with me here,' said the Emperor. 'Drink some tea. It must be a strange thing, if it is true, to see a man fly. You must have time to think of it, even as I must have time to prepare myself for the sight.'

They drank tea.

'Please,' said the servant at last, 'or he will be gone.'

The Emperor rose thoughtfully. 'Now you may show me what you have seen.'

They walked into a garden, across a meadow of grass, over a small bridge, through a grove of trees, and up a tiny hill.

'There!' said the servant.

The Emperor looked into the sky.

And in the sky, laughing so high that you could hardly hear him laugh, was a man; and the man was clothed in bright papers and reeds to make wings and a beautiful yellow tail, and he was soaring all about like the largest bird in a universe of birds, like a new dragon in a land of ancient dragons.

The man called down to them from high in the cool winds of morning. 'I fly, I fly!'

The servant waved to him. 'Yes, yes!'

The Emperor Yuan did not move. Instead he looked at the Great Wall of China now taking shape out of the farthest mist in the green hills, that splendid snake of stones which writhed with majesty across the entire land. That wonderful wall which had protected them for a timeless time from enemy hordes and preserved peace for years without number. He saw the town, nestled to itself by a river and a road and a hill, beginning to waken.

'Tell me,' he said to his servant, 'has anyone else seen this flying man?'

'I am the only one, Excellency,' said the servant, smiling at the sky, waving.

The Emperor watched the heavens another minute and then said, 'Call him down to me.'

'Ho, come down, come down! The Emperor wishes to see you!' called the servant, hands cupped to his shouting mouth.

The Emperor glanced in all directions while the flying man soared down the morning wind. He saw a farmer, early in his fields, watching the sky, and he noted where the farmer stood.

The flying man alit with a rustle of paper and a creak of bamboo reeds. He came proudly to the Emperor, clumsy in his rig, at last bowing before the old man.

'What have you done?' demanded the Emperor.

'I have flown in the sky, Your Excellency,' replied the man.

'What *have* you done?' said the Emperor again.

'I have just told you!' cried the flyer.

'You have told me nothing at all.' The Emperor reached out a thin hand to touch the pretty paper and the birdlike keel of the apparatus. It smelled cool, of the wind.

'Is it not beautiful, Excellency?'

'Yes, too beautiful.'

'It is the only one in the world!' smiled the man. 'And I am the inventor.'

'The *only* one in the world?'

'I swear it!'

'Who else knows of this?'

'No one. Not even my wife, who would think me mad with the sun. She thought I was making a kite. I rose in the night and walked to the cliffs far away. And when the morning breezes blew and the sun rose, I gathered my courage, Excellency, and leaped from the cliff. I flew! But my wife does not know of it.'

'Well for her, then,' said the Emperor. 'Come along.'

They walked back to the great house. The sun was full in the sky now, and the smell of the grass was refreshing. The Emperor, the servant, and the flyer paused within the huge garden.

The Emperor clapped his hands. 'Ho, guards!'

The guards came running.

'Hold this man.'

The guards seized the flyer.

'Call the executioner,' said the Emperor.

'What's this!' cried the flyer, bewildered. 'What have I done?' He began to weep, so that the beautiful paper apparatus rustled.

'Here is the man who has made a certain machine,' said the Emperor, 'and yet asks us what he has created. He does not know himself. It is only necessary that he create, without knowing why he has done so, or what this thing will do.'

The executioner came running with a sharp silver axe. He stood with his naked, large-muscled arms ready, his face covered with a serene white mask.

'One moment,' said the Emperor. He turned to a nearby table upon which sat a machine that he himself had created. The Emperor took a tiny golden key from his own neck. He fitted this key to the tiny, delicate machine and wound it up. Then he set the machine going.

The machine was a garden of metal and jewels. Set in motion, birds sang in tiny metal trees, wolves walked through miniature forests, and tiny people ran in and out of sun and shadow, fanning themselves with miniature fans, listening to the tiny emerald birds, and standing by impossibly small but tinkling fountains.

'Is *it* not beautiful?' said the Emperor. 'If you asked me what I have done here, I could answer you well. I have made birds sing. I have made forests murmur. I have set people to walking in this woodland, enjoying the leaves and shadows and songs. That is what I have done.'

'But, oh, Emperor!' pleaded the flyer, on his knees, the tears pouring down his face. 'I have done a similar thing! I have found beauty. I have flown on the morning wind. I have looked down on all the sleeping houses and gardens. I have smelled the sea and even *seen* it, beyond the hills, from my high place. And I have soared like a bird; oh, I cannot say how beautiful it is up there, in the sky, with the wind about me, the wind blowing me here like a feather, there like a fan, the way the sky smells in the morning! And how free one feels! *That* is beautiful, Emperor, that is beautiful too!'

'Yes,' said the Emperor sadly, 'I know it must be true. For I felt my heart move with you in the air and I wondered: what is it like? How does it feel? How do the distant pools look from so high? And how my houses and servants! Like ants? And how the distant towns not yet awake?'

'Then spare me!'

'But there are times,' said the Emperor, more sadly still, 'when one must lose a little beauty if one is to keep what little beauty one already has. I do not fear you, yourself, but I fear another man.'

'What man?'

'Some other man who, seeing you, will build a thing of bright papers and bamboo like this. But the other man will have an evil face and an evil heart, and the beauty will be gone. It is this man I fear.'

'Why? Why?'

'Who is to say that some day just such a man, in just such an apparatus of paper and reed, might not fly in the sky and drop huge stones upon the Great Wall of China?' said the Emperor.

No one moved or said a word.

'Off with his head,' said the Emperor.

The executioner whirled his silver axe.

'Burn the kite and the inventor's body and bury their ashes together,' said the Emperor.

The servants retreated to obey.

The Emperor turned to his hand-servant, who had seen the man flying. 'Hold your tongue. It was all a dream, a most sorrowful and beautiful dream. And that farmer in the distant field who also saw, tell him it would pay him to consider it only a vision. If ever the word passes around, you and the farmer die within the hour.'

'You are merciful, Emperor.'

'No, not merciful,' said the old man. Beyond the garden wall he saw the guards burning the beautiful machine of paper and reeds that smelled of the morning wind. He saw the dark smoke climb into the sky. 'No, only very much bewildered and afraid.' He saw the guards digging a tiny pit wherein to bury the ashes. 'What is the life of one man against those of a million others? I must take solace from that thought.'

He took the key from its chain about his neck and once more wound up the beautiful miniature garden. He stood looking out across the land at the Great Wall, the peaceful town, the green fields, the rivers and streams. He sighed. The tiny garden whirred its hidden and delicate machinery and set itself in motion; tiny people walked in forests, tiny foxes loped through sun-speckled glades in beautiful shining pelts, and among the tiny trees flew little bits of high song and bright blue and yellow colour, flying, flying, flying in that small sky.

'Oh,' said the Emperor, closing his eyes, 'look at the birds, look at the birds!'

Ray Bradbury

115

A martian sends a postcard home

Caxtons are mechanical birds with many wings
and some are treasured for their markings—

they cause the eyes to melt
or the body to shriek without pain.

I have never seen one fly, but
sometimes they perch on the hand.

Mist is when the sky is tired of flight
and rests its soft machine on ground:

then the world is dim and bookish
like engravings under tissue paper.

Rain is when the earth is television.
It has the property of making colours darker.

Model T is a room with the lock inside—
a key is turned to free the world

for movement, so quick there is a film
to watch for anything missed.

But time is tied to the wrist
or kept in a box, ticking with impatience.

In homes, a haunted apparatus sleeps,
that snores when you pick it up.

If the ghost cries, they carry it
to their lips and soothe it to sleep

with sounds. And yet, they wake it up
deliberately, by tickling with a finger.

Only the young are allowed to suffer
openly. Adults go to a punishment room

with water but nothing to eat.
They lock the door and suffer the noises

alone. No one is exempt
and everyone's pain has a different smell.

At night, when all the colours die,
they hide in pairs

and read about themselves—
in colour, with their eyelids shut.

Craig Raine

Activities

Geography lesson

1 Why is this poem called *Geography lesson?*
2 Suppose you had to give it a different title. What would you call it and why?

Writing

You can use the pattern of this poem to write about different subjects. The main features are:

- three verses
- in each verse you move further away from the thing you are talking about
- as you move away you see it in a different way
- in the last verse you get a new understanding
- there are repeated lines

The watchman

At the end of the story we don't really know whether it was the same woman or not. Suppose it was. She has returned to the tank and remembers that evening when she spoke to the watchman. Why doesn't she recognise him now? Think about this and then make up *her* version of the story – as she tells it to her oldest daughter.
Either: Write as if you are the woman talking.
Or   : Write the script of the conversation they have.

The new place

Reading the scene

Work with a partner.

1 Read the scene through on your own.
2 Discuss it. Decide:
   a) what the characters are like,
   b) who should play each part.
3 Practise reading the scene.
4 When you have finished, discuss how it went and how it could be improved.
5 Try it again until you are satisfied with it.

Writing

Write two character descriptions:

   the man as seen by the welfare woman
   the welfare woman as seen by the man

The shaft

First impressions
Read the story. Jot down your first impressions of:

1   Harry and Willy
2   Their wives
3   Williamson
4   Life as a miner

Discussion

Discuss your notes with a partner.

Writing

Now write about the characters in the story, using the notes you have made.

The flying machine

Writing

1   Imagine that you are the Emperor Yuan. Describe your thoughts and feelings, and explain your actions in this story.
2   Suppose someone in a century before ours had had the power to destroy an invention and remove all traces of its existence. Tell the story of what happened. Your story can be serious or funny, or a mixture of the two. Think of an invention yourself, or choose one from this list: television, nuclear weapons, the motor car, the wheel, writing, computers, electricity, false teeth.

A martian sends a postcard home

Discussion

1   What has the martian seen?
2   Craig Raine cannot really know how a martian would react to life on earth. So what is the point of the poem?

Writing

How do you suppose the martian would report on other aspects of human life, like school, or a supermarket, or a holiday resort? Choose an aspect of human life and then write *The martian's second postcard home.*

Some are more equal than others

The stolen party

As soon as she arrived she went straight to the kitchen to see if the monkey was there. It was: what a relief! She wouldn't have liked to admit that her mother had been right. *Monkeys at a birthday?* her mother had sneered. *Get away with you, believing any nonsense you're told!* She was cross, but not because of the monkey, the girl thought; it's just because of the party.

'I don't like you going,' she told her. 'It's a rich people's party.'

'Rich people go to Heaven too,' said the girl, who studied religion at school.

'Get away with Heaven,' said the mother. 'The problem with you, young lady, is that you like to fart higher than your ass.'

The girl didn't approve of the way her mother spoke. She was barely nine, and one of the best in her class.

'I'm going because I've been invited,' she said. 'And I've been invited because Luciana is my friend. So there.'

'Ah yes, your friend,' her mother grumbled. She paused. 'Listen, Rosaura,' she said at last. 'That one's not your friend. You know what you are to them? The maid's daughter, that's what.'

Rosaura blinked hard: she wasn't going to cry. Then she yelled: 'Shut up! You know nothing about being friends!'

Every afternoon she used to go to Luciana's house and they would both finish their homework while Rosaura's mother did the cleaning. They had their tea in the kitchen and they told each other secrets. Rosaura loved everything in the big house, and she also loved the people who lived there.

'I'm going because it will be the most lovely party in the whole world, Luciana told me it would. There will be a magician, and he will bring a monkey and everything.'

The mother swung around to take a good look at her child, and pompously put her hands on her hips.

'Monkeys at a birthday?' she said. 'Get away with you, believing any nonsense you're told!'

Rosaura was deeply offended. She thought it unfair of her mother to accuse other people of being liars simply because they were rich. Rosaura too wanted to be rich, of course. If one day she managed to live in a beautiful palace, would her mother stop loving her? She felt very sad. She wanted to go to that party more than anything else in the world.

'I'll die if I don't go,' she whispered, almost without moving her lips.

And she wasn't sure whether she had been heard, but on the morning of the party she discovered that her mother had starched her Christmas dress. And in the afternoon, after washing her hair, her mother rinsed it in apple vinegar so that it would be all nice and shiny. Before going out, Rosaura admired herself in the mirror, with her white dress and glossy hair, and thought she looked terribly pretty.

Señora Ines also seemed to notice. As soon as she saw her, she said:

'How lovely you look today, Rosaura.'

Rosaura gave her starched skirt a slight toss with her hands and walked into the party with a firm step. She said hello to Luciana and asked about the monkey. Luciana put on a secretive look and whispered into Rosaura's ear: 'He's in the kitchen. But don't tell anyone, because it's a surprise.'

Rosaura wanted to make sure. Carefully she entered the kitchen and there she saw it: deep in thought, inside its cage. It looked so funny that the girl stood there for a while, watching it, and later, every so often, she would slip out of the party unseen and go and admire it. Rosaura was the only one allowed into the kitchen. Señora Ines had said: 'You yes, but not the others, they're much too boisterous, they might break something.' Rosaura had never broken anything. She even managed the jug of orange juice, carrying it from the kitchen into the dining-room. She held it carefully and didn't spill a single drop. And Señora Ines had said: 'Are you sure you can manage a jug as big as that?' Of course she could manage. She wasn't a butterfingers, like the others. Like that blonde girl with the bow in her hair. As soon as she saw Rosaura, the girl with the bow had said:

'And you? Who are you?'

'I'm a friend of Luciana,' said Rosaura.

'No,' said the girl with the bow, 'you are not a friend of Luciana because I'm her cousin and I know all her friends. And I don't know you.'

'So what,' said Rosaura. 'I come here every afternoon with my mother and we do our homework together.'

'You and your mother do your homework together?' asked the girl, laughing.

'I and Luciana do our homework together,' said Rosaura, very seriously.

The girl with the bow shrugged her shoulders.

'That's not being friends,' she said. 'Do you go to school together?'

'No.'

'So where do you know her from?' said the girl, getting impatient.

Rosaura remembered her mother's words perfectly. She took a deep breath.

'I'm the daughter of the employee,' she said.

Her mother had said very clearly: 'If someone asks, you say you're the daughter of the employee; that's all.' She also told her to add: 'And proud of it.' But Rosaura thought that never in her life would she dare say something of the sort.

'What employee?' said the girl with the bow. 'Employee in a shop?'

'No,' said Rosaura angrily. 'My mother doesn't sell anything in any shop, so there.'

'So how come she's an employee?' said the girl with the bow.

Just then Señora Ines arrived saying *shh shh*, and asked Rosaura if she wouldn't mind helping serve out the hot-dogs, as she knew the house so much better than the others.

'See?' said Rosaura to the girl with the bow, and when no one was looking she kicked her in the shin.

Apart from the girl with the bow, all the others were delightful. The one she liked best was Luciana, with her golden birthday crown; and then the boys. Rosaura won the sack race, and nobody managed to catch her when they played tag. When they split into two teams to play charades, all the boys wanted her for their side. Rosaura felt she had never been so happy in all her life.

But the best was still to come. The best came after Luciana blew out the candles. First the cake. Señora Ines had asked her to help pass the cake around, and Rosaura had enjoyed the task immensely, because everyone called out to her, shouting 'Me, me!' Rosaura remembered a story in which there was a queen who had the power of life or death over her subjects. She had always loved that, having the power of life or death. To Luciana and the boys she gave the largest pieces, and to the girl with the bow she gave a slice so thin one could see through it.

After the cake came the magician, tall and bony, with a fine red cape. A true magician: he could untie handkerchiefs by blowing on them and make a chain with links that had no openings. He could guess what cards were pulled out from a pack, and the monkey was his assistant. He called the monkey 'partner.' 'Let's see here, partner,' he would say, 'Turn over a card.' And, 'Don't run away, partner: time to work now.'

The final trick was wonderful. One of the children had to hold the monkey in his arms and the magician said he would make him disappear.

'What, the boy?' they all shouted.

'No, the monkey!' shouted back the magician.

Rosaura thought that this was truly the most amusing party in the whole world.

The magician asked a small fat boy to come and help, but the small fat boy got frightened almost at once and dropped the monkey on the floor. The magician picked him up carefully, whispered something in his ear, and the monkey nodded almost as if he understood.

'You mustn't be so unmanly, my friend,' the magician said to the fat boy.

'What's unmanly?' said the fat boy.

The magician turned around as if to look for spies.

'A sissy,' said the magician. 'Go sit down.'

Then he stared at all the faces, one by one. Rosaura felt her heart tremble.

'You, with the Spanish eyes,' said the magician. And everyone saw that he was pointing at her.

She wasn't afraid. Neither holding the monkey, nor when the magician made him vanish; not even when, at the end, the magician flung his red cape over Rosaura's head and uttered a few magic words...and the monkey reappeared, chattering happily, in her arms. The children clapped furiously. And before Rosaura returned to her seat, the magician said:

'Thank you very much, my little countess.'

She was so pleased with the compliment that a while later, when her mother came to fetch her, that was the first thing she told her.

'I helped the magician and he said to me, "Thank you very much, my little countess."'

It was strange because up to then Rosaura had thought that she was angry with her mother. All along Rosaura had imagined that she would say to her: 'See that the monkey wasn't a lie?' But instead she was so thrilled that she told her mother all about the wonderful magician.

Her mother tapped her on the head and said: 'So now we're a countess!'

But one could see that she was beaming.

And now they both stood in the entrance, because a moment ago Señora Ines, smiling, had said: 'Please wait here a second.'

Her mother suddenly seemed worried.

'What is it?' she asked Rosaura.

'What is what?' said Rosaura. 'It's nothing; she just wants to get the presents for those who are leaving, see?'

She pointed at the fat boy and at a girl with pigtails who were also waiting there, next to their mothers. And she explained about the presents. She knew, because she had been watching those who left before her. When one of the girls was about to leave, Señora Ines would give her a bracelet. When a boy left, Señora Ines gave him a yo-yo. Rosaura preferred the yo-yo because

124

it sparkled, but she didn't mention that to her mother. Her mother might have said: 'So why don't you ask for one, you blockhead?' That's what her mother was like. Rosaura didn't feel like explaining that she'd be horribly ashamed to be the odd one out. Instead she said:

'I was the best-behaved at the party.'

And she said no more because Señora Ines came out into the hall with two bags, one pink and one blue.

First she went up to the fat boy, gave him a yo-yo out of the blue bag, and the fat boy left with his mother. Then she went up to the girl and gave her a bracelet out of the pink bag, and the girl with the pigtails left as well.

Finally she came up to Rosaura and her mother. She had a big smile on her face and Rosaura liked that. Señora Ines looked down at her, then looked up at her mother, and then said something that made Rosaura proud:

'What a marvellous daughter you have, Herminia.'

For an instant, Rosaura thought that she'd give her two presents: the bracelet and the yo-yo. Señora Ines bent down as if about to look for something. Rosaura also leaned forward, stretching out her arm. But she never completed the movement.

Señora Ines didn't look in the pink bag. Nor did she look in the blue bag. Instead she rummaged in her purse. In her hand appeared two bills.

'You really and truly earned this,' she said handing them over. 'Thank you for all your help, my pet.'

Rosaura felt her arms stiffen, stick close to her body, and then she noticed her mother's hand on her shoulder. Instinctively she pressed herself against her mother's body. That was all. Except her eyes. Rosaura's eyes had a cold, clear look that fixed itself on Señora Ines's face.

Señora Ines, motionless, stood there with her hand outstretched. As if she didn't dare draw it back. As if the slightest change might shatter an infinitely delicate balance.

Liliana Heker

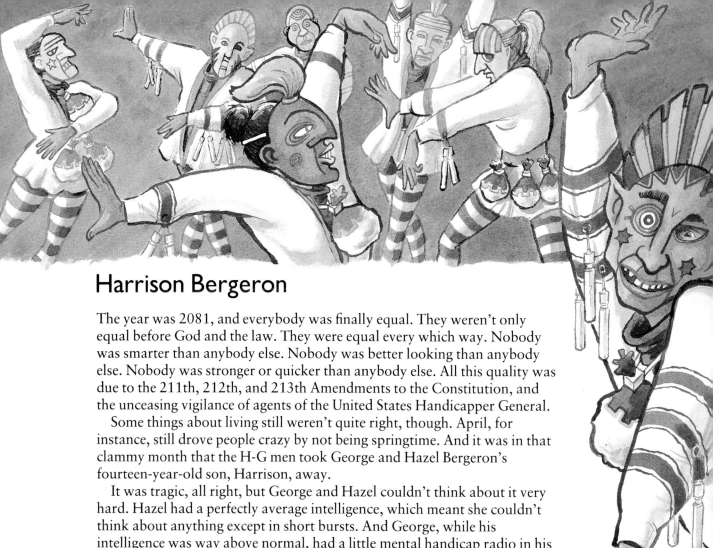

Harrison Bergeron

The year was 2081, and everybody was finally equal. They weren't only equal before God and the law. They were equal every which way. Nobody was smarter than anybody else. Nobody was better looking than anybody else. Nobody was stronger or quicker than anybody else. All this quality was due to the 211th, 212th, and 213th Amendments to the Constitution, and the unceasing vigilance of agents of the United States Handicapper General.

Some things about living still weren't quite right, though. April, for instance, still drove people crazy by not being springtime. And it was in that clammy month that the H-G men took George and Hazel Bergeron's fourteen-year-old son, Harrison, away.

It was tragic, all right, but George and Hazel couldn't think about it very hard. Hazel had a perfectly average intelligence, which meant she couldn't think about anything except in short bursts. And George, while his intelligence was way above normal, had a little mental handicap radio in his ear. He was required by law to wear it at all times. It was tuned to a government transmitter. Every twenty seconds or so, the transmitter would send out some sharp noise to keep people like George from taking unfair advantage of their brains.

George and Hazel were watching television. There were tears on Hazel's cheeks, but she'd forgotten for the moment what they were about.

On the television screen were ballerinas.

A buzzer sounded in George's head. His thoughts fled in panic, like bandits from a burglar-alarm.

'That was a real pretty dance, that dance they just did,' said Hazel.

'Huh?' said George.

'That dance – it was nice,' said Hazel.

'Yup,' said George. He tried to think a little about the ballerinas. They weren't really very good – no better than anybody else would have been, anyway. They were burdened with sashweights and bags of birdshot, and their faces were masked, so that no one, seeing a free and graceful gesture or a pretty face, would feel like something the cat dragged in. George was toying with the vague notion that maybe dancers shouldn't be handicapped. But he didn't get very far with it before another noise in his ear radio scattered his thoughts.

George winced. So did two out of the eight ballerinas.

Hazel saw him wince. Having no mental handicap herself, she had to ask

George what the latest sound had been.

'Sounded like somebody hitting a milk bottle with a ball peen hammer,' said George.

'I'd think it would be real interesting, hearing all the different sounds,' said Hazel, a little envious. 'All the things they think up.'

'Um,' said George.

'Only, if I was Handicapper General, you know what I would do?' said Hazel. Hazel, as a matter of fact, bore a strong resemblance to the Handicapper General, a woman named Diana Moon Glampers. 'If I was Diana Moon Glampers,' said Hazel, 'I'd have chimes on Sunday – just chimes. Kind of in honour of religion.'

'I could think, if it was just chimes,' said George.

'Well – maybe make 'em real loud,' said Hazel. 'I think I'd make a good Handicapper General.'

'Good as anybody else,' said George.

'Who knows better'n I do what normal is?' said Hazel.

'Right,' said George. He began to think glimmeringly about his abnormal son who was now in jail, about Harrison, but a twenty-one-gun salute in his head stopped that.

'Boy,' said Hazel, 'that was a doozy, wasn't it?'

It was such a doozy that George was white and trembling, and tears stood on the rims of his red eyes. Two of the eight ballerinas had collapsed to the studio floor, were holding their temples.

'All of a sudden you look so tired,' said Hazel. 'Why don't you stretch out on the sofa, so's you can rest your handicap bag on the pillows, honeybunch.' She was referring to the forty-seven pounds of birdshot in a canvas bag, which was padlocked around George's neck. 'Go on and rest the bag for a little while,' she said. 'I don't care if you're not equal to me for a while.'

George weighed the bag with his hands. 'I don't mind it,' he said. 'I don't notice it any more. It's just a part of me.'

'You been so tired lately – kind of worn out,' said Hazel. 'If there was just some way we could make a little hole in the bottom of the bag, and just take out a few of them lead balls. Just a few.'

'Two years in prison and two thousand dollars fine for every ball I took out,' said George. 'I don't call that a bargain.'

'If you could just take a few out when you came home from work,' said Hazel. 'I mean – you don't compete with anybody around here. You just sit around.'

'If I tried to get away with it,' said George, 'then other people'd get away with it – and pretty soon we'd be right back to the dark ages again, with everybody competing against everybody else. You wouldn't like that, would you?'

'I'd hate it,' said Hazel.

'There you are,' said George. 'The minute people start cheating on laws, what do you think happens to society?'

If Hazel hadn't been able to come up with an answer to this question, George couldn't have supplied one. A siren was going off in his head.

'Reckon it'd fall all apart,' said Hazel.

'What would?' said George blankly.

'Society,' said Hazel uncertainly. 'Wasn't that what you just said?'

'Who knows?' said George.

The television programme was suddenly interrupted for a news bulletin. It wasn't clear at first as to what the bulletin was about, since the announcer, like all announcers, had a serious speech impediment. For about half a minute, and in a state of high excitement, the announcer tried to say, 'Ladies and gentlemen –'

He finally gave up, handed the bulletin to a ballerina to read.

'That's all right –' Hazel said of the announcer, 'he tried. That's the big thing. He tried to do the best he could with what God gave him. He should get a nice raise for trying so hard.'

'Ladies and gentlemen –' said the ballerina, reading the bulletin. She must have been extraordinarily beautiful, because the mask she wore was hideous. And it was easy to see that she was the strongest and most graceful of all the dancers, for her handicap bags were as big as those worn by two-hundred-pound men.

And she had to apologise at once for her voice, which was a very unfair voice for a woman to use. Her voice was a warm, luminous, timeless melody. 'Excuse me –' she said, and she began again, making her voice absolutely uncompetitive.

'Harrison Bergeron, age fourteen,' she said in a grackle squawk, 'has just escaped from jail, where he was held on suspicion of plotting to overthrow the government. He is a genius and an athlete, is under-handicapped, and should be regarded as extremely dangerous.'

A police photograph of Harrison Bergeron was flashed on the screen – upside-down, then sideways, upside-down again, then right side up. The picture showed the full length of Harrison against a background calibrated in feet and inches. He was exactly seven feet tall.

The rest of Harrison's appearance was Halloween and hardware. Nobody had ever borne heavier handicaps. He had outgrown hindrances faster than the H-G men could think them up. Instead of a little ear radio for a mental handicap, he wore a tremendous pair of earphones, and spectacles with thick wavy lenses. The spectacles were intended to make him not only half blind, but to give him whanging headaches besides.

Scrap metal was hung all over him. Ordinarily, there was a certain symmetry, a military neatness to the handicaps issued to strong people, but Harrison looked like a walking junkyard. In the race of life, Harrison carried three hundred pounds.

And to offset his good looks, the H-G men required that he wear at all times a red rubber ball for a nose, keep his eye-brows shaved off, and cover his even white teeth with black caps at snaggle-tooth random.

'If you see this boy,' said the ballerina, 'do not – I repeat, do not – try to reason with him.'

There was the shriek of a door being torn from its hinges.

Screams and barking cries of consternation came from the television set. The photograph of Harrison Bergeron on the screen jumped again and again, as though dancing to the tune of an earthquake.

George Bergeron correctly identified the earthquake, and well he might have – for many was the time his own home had danced to the same crashing tune. 'My God –' said George, 'that must be Harrison!'

The realisation was blasted from his mind instantly by the sound of an automobile collision in his head.

When George could open his eyes again, the photograph of Harrison was gone. A living, breathing Harrison filled the screen.

Clanking, clownish, and huge, Harrison stood in the centre of the studio. The knob of the uprooted studio door was still in his hand. Ballerinas, technicians, musicians, and announcers cowered on their knees before him, expecting to die.

'I am the Emperor!' cried Harrison. 'Do you hear? I am the Emperor! Everybody must do what I say at once!' He stamped his foot and the studio shook.

'Even as I stand here –' he bellowed, 'crippled, hobbled, sickened – I am a greater ruler than any man who ever lived! Now watch me become what I *can* become!'

Harrison tore the straps of his handicap harness like wet tissue paper, tore straps guaranteed to support five thousand pounds.

Harrison's scrap-iron handicaps crashed to the floor.

Harrison thrust his thumbs under the bar of the padlock that secured his head harness. The bar snapped like celery. Harrison smashed his headphones and spectacles against the wall.

He flung away his rubber-ball nose, revealed a man that would have awed Thor, the god of thunder.

'I shall now select my Empress!' he said, looking down on the cowering people. 'Let the first woman who dares rise to her feet claim her mate and her throne!'

A moment passed, and then a ballerina arose, swaying like a willow.

Harrison plucked the mental handicap from her ear, snapped off her physical handicaps with marvellous delicacy. Last of all, he removed her mask.

She was blindingly beautiful.

'Now –' said Harrison, taking her hand, 'shall we show the people the meaning of the word dance? Music!' he commanded.

The musicians scrambled back into their chairs, and Harrison stripped them of their handicaps, too. 'Play your best,' he told them, 'and I'll make you barons and dukes and earls.'

The music began. It was normal at first – cheap, silly, false. But Harrison snatched two musicians from their chairs, waved them like batons as he sang the music as he wanted it played. He slammed them back into their chairs.

The music began again and was much improved.

Harrison and his Empress merely listened to the music for a while – listened gravely, as though synchronising their heart beats with it.

They shifted their weights to their toes.

Harrison placed his big hands on the girl's tiny waist, letting her sense the weightlessness that would soon be hers.

And then, in an explosion of joy and grace, into the air they sprang!

Not only were the laws of the land abandoned, but the law of gravity and the laws of motion as well.

They reeled, whirled, swivelled, flounced, capered, gambolled, and spun.

They leaped like deer on the moon.

The studio ceiling was thirty feet high, but each leap brought the dancers nearer to it.

It became their obvious intention to kiss the ceiling.

They kissed it.

And then, neutralising gravity with love and pure will, they remained suspended in air inches below the ceiling, and they kissed each other for a long, long time.

It was then that Diana Moon Glampers, the Handicapper General, came into the studio with a double-barrelled ten-gauge shotgun. She fired twice, and the Emperor and the Empress were dead before they hit the floor.

Diana Moon Glampers loaded the gun again. She aimed it at the musicians and told them they had ten seconds to get their handicaps back on.

It was then that the Bergerons' television tube burned out.

Hazel turned to comment about the blackout to George. But George had gone out into the kitchen for a can of beer.

George came back in with the beer, paused while a handicap signal shook him up. And then he sat down again. 'You been crying?' he said to Hazel.

'Yup,' she said.

'What about?' he said.

'I forget,' she said. 'Something real sad on television.'

'What was it?' he said.

'It's all kind of mixed up in my mind,' said Hazel.

'Forget sad things,' said George.

'I always do,' said Hazel.

'That's my girl,' said George. He winced. There was the sound of a rivetting gun in his head.

'Gee – I could tell that one was a doozy,' said Hazel.

'You can say that again,' said George.

'Gee –' said Hazel, 'I could tell that one was a doozy.'

Kurt Vonnegut Junior

After you, my dear Alphonse

Mrs Wilson was just taking the gingerbread out of the oven when she heard Johnny outside talking to someone.

'Johnny,' she called, 'you're late. Come in and get your lunch.'

'Just a minute, Mother,' Johnny said. 'After you, my dear Alphonse.'

'After *you*, my dear Alphonse,' another voice said.

'No, after *you*, my dear Alphonse,' Johnny said.

Mrs Wilson opened the door. 'Johnny,' she said, 'you come in this minute and get your lunch. You can play after you've eaten.'

Johnny came in after her, slowly. 'Mother,' he said, 'I brought Boyd home for lunch with me.'

'Boyd?' Mrs Wilson thought for a moment. 'I don't believe I've met Boyd. Bring him in, dear, since you've invited him. Lunch is ready.'

'Boyd!' Johnny yelled. 'Hey, Boyd, come on in!'

'I'm coming. Just got to unload this stuff.'

'Well, hurry, or my mother'll be sore.'

'Johnny, that's not very polite to either your friend or your mother,' Mrs Wilson said. 'Come sit down, Boyd.'

As she turned to show Boyd where to sit, she saw he was a Negro boy, smaller than Johnny but about the same age. His arms were loaded with split kindling wood. 'Where'll I put this stuff, Johnny?' he asked.

Mrs Wilson turned to Johnny. 'Johnny,' she said, 'what did you make Boyd do? What is that wood?'

'Dead Japanese,' Johnny said mildly. 'We stand them in the ground and run over them with tanks.'

'How do you do, Mrs Wilson?' Boyd said.

'How do you do, Boyd? You shouldn't let Johnny make you carry all that wood. Sit down now and eat lunch, both of you.'

'Why shouldn't he carry the wood, Mother? It's his wood. We got it at his place.'

'Johnny,' Mrs Wilson said, 'go on and eat your lunch.'

'Sure,' Johnny said. He held out the dish of scrambled eggs to Boyd. 'After you, my dear Alphonse.'

'After *you*, my dear Alphonse,' Boyd said.

'After *you*, my dear Alphonse,' Johnny said. They began to giggle.

'Are you hungry, Boyd?' Mrs Wilson asked.

'Yes, Mrs Wilson.'

'Well, don't let Johnny stop you. He always fusses about eating, so you just see that you get a good lunch. There's plenty of food here for you to have all you want.'

'Thank you, Mrs Wilson.'

'Come on, Alphonse,' Johnny said. He pushed half the scrambled eggs on to Boyd's plate. Boyd watched while Mrs Wilson put a dish of stewed tomatoes beside his plate.

'Boyd don't eat tomatoes, do you, Boyd?' Johnny said.

'*Doesn't* eat tomatoes, Johnny. And just because you don't like them, don't say that about Boyd. Boyd will eat *anything*.'

'Bet he won't,' Johnny said, attacking his scrambled eggs.

'Boyd wants to grow up and be a big strong man so he can work hard,' Mrs Wilson said. 'I'll bet Boyd's father eats stewed tomatoes.'

'My father eats anything he wants to,' Boyd said.

'So does mine,' Johnny said. 'Sometimes he doesn't eat hardly anything. He's a little guy, though. Wouldn't hurt a flea.'

'Mine's a little guy, too,' Boyd said.

'I'll bet he's strong, though,' Mrs Wilson said. She hesitated. 'Does he . . . work?'

'Sure,' Johnny said. 'Boyd's father works in a factory.'

'There, you see?' Mrs Wilson said. 'And he certainly has to be strong to do that – all that lifting and carrying at a factory.'

'Boyd's father doesn't have to,' Johnny said. 'He's a foreman.'

Mrs Wilson felt defeated. 'What does your mother do, Boyd?'

'My mother?' Boyd was surprised. 'She takes care of us kids.'

'Oh. She doesn't work, then?'

'Why should she?' Johnny said through a mouthful of eggs. 'You don't work.'

'You really don't want any stewed tomatoes, Boyd?'

'No, thank you, Mrs Wilson,' Boyd said.

'No, thank you, Mrs Wilson, no, thank you, Mrs Wilson, no thank you, Mrs Wilson,' Johnny said. 'Boyd's sister's going to work, though. She's going to be a teacher.'

'That's a very fine attitude for her to have, Boyd.' Mrs Wilson restrained an impulse to pat Boyd on the head. 'I imagine you're all very proud of her?'

'I guess so,' Boyd said.

'What about all your other brothers and sisters? I guess all of you want to make just as much of yourselves as you can.'

'There's only me and Jean,' Boyd said. 'I don't know yet what I want to be when I grow up.'

'We're going to be tank drivers, Boyd and me,' Johnny said, 'Zoom.' Mrs Wilson caught Boyd's glass of milk as Johnny's napkin ring, suddenly transformed into a tank, plowed heavily across the table.

'Look, Johnny,' Boyd said. 'Here's a foxhole. I'm shooting at you.'

Mrs Wilson, with the speed born of long experience, took the gingerbread off the shelf and placed it carefully between the tank and the foxhole.

'Now eat as much as you want to, Boyd,' she said. 'I want to see you get filled up.'

'Boyd eats a lot, but not as much as I do,' Johnny said. 'I'm bigger than he is.'

'You're not much bigger,' Boyd said. 'I can beat you running.'

Mrs Wilson took a deep breath. 'Boyd,' she said. Both boys turned to her. 'Boyd, Johnny has some suits that are a little too small for him, and a winter coat. It's not new, of course, but there's lots of wear in it still. And I have a few dresses that your mother or sister could probably use. Your mother can make them into lots of things for all of you, and I'd be very happy to give them to you. Suppose before you leave I make up a big bundle and then you and Johnny can take it over to your mother right away . . .' Her voice trailed off as she saw Boyd's puzzled expression.

'But I have plenty of clothes, thank you,' he said. 'And I don't think my mother knows how to sew very well, and anyway I guess we buy about everything we need. Thank you very much, though.'

'We don't have time to carry that old stuff around, Mother,' Johnny said. 'We got to play tanks with the kids today.'

Mrs Wilson lifted the plate of gingerbread off the table as Boyd was about to take another piece. 'There are many little boys like you, Boyd, who would be very grateful for the clothes someone was kind enough to give them.'

'Boyd will take them if you want him to, Mother,' Johnny said.

'I didn't mean to make you mad, Mrs Wilson,' Boyd said.

'Don't think I'm angry, Boyd. I'm just disappointed in you, that's all. Now let's not say anything more about it.'

She began clearing the plates off the table, and Johnny took Boyd's hand and pulled him to the door. 'Bye, Mother,' Johnny said. Boyd stood for a minute, staring at Mrs Wilson's back.

'After you, my dear Alphonse,' Johnny said, holding the door open.

'Is your mother still mad?' Mrs Wilson heard Boyd ask in a low voice.

'I don't know,' Johnny said. 'She's screwy sometimes.'

'So's mine,' Boyd said. He hesitated. 'After *you*, my dear Alphonse.'

Shirley Jackson

The qualification

wurk aw yir life
nuthnty show
pit oanthi nyuze
same awl drivl

yoonyin bashn
wurkir bashn
lord this
sir soan soa thaht

shood hearma boay
sayzwi need gunz
an armd revalooshn
nuthn else wurks

awright fur him thoa
uppit thi yooni
tok aw yi like therr
thats whit its fur

Tom Leonard

Girls can we educate we dads?

Listn the male chauvinist in mi dad –
a girl walkin night street mus be bad.
He don't say, the world's a free place
for a girl to keep her unmolested space.
Instead he say – a girl is a girl.

He say a girl walkin swingin hips about
call boys fi look and shout.
He don't say, if a girl have style
she want to say, look
I okay from top to foot.
Instead he say – a girl is a girl.

Listn the male chauvinist in mi dad –
a girl too laughy-laughy look too easy and glad
jus like a girl too looky-looky roun
wi get a pretty satan at her side.
He don't say – a girl full-a life
wi don't want fi stifle her jive.
Instead he say – a girl is a girl.

James Berry

Men talk

Women
Rabbit rabbit rabbit women
Tattle and titter
Women prattle
Women waffle and witter

Men Talk. Men Talk.

Women into Girl Talk
About Women's Trouble
Trivia 'n' Small Talk
They yap and they babble

Men Talk. Men Talk.

Women yatter
Women chatter
Women chew the fat, women spill the beans
Women aint been takin'
The oh-so Good Advice in them
Women's Magazines.

A Man Likes A Good Listener.

Oh yeah
I like A Woman
Who likes me enough
Not to nitpick
Not to nag and
Not to interrupt 'cause I call that treason
A woman with the Good Grace
To be struck dumb
By me Sweet Reason. Yes –
A Man Likes a Good Listener

A Real
Man
Likes a Real Good Listener

Women yap yap yap
Verbal Diarrhoea is a Female Disease
Woman she spread she rumours round she
Like Philadelphia Cream Cheese.

Oh
Bossy Women Gossip
Girlish Women Giggle
Women natter, women nag
Women niggle niggle niggle
Men Talk.

Men
Think First, Speak Later
Men Talk.

Liz Lochhead

135

Activities

The stolen party

Questions

1 Why is the story called *The stolen party*?
2 All through the story, we follow Rosaura's thoughts and feelings. How does this affect what we get out of the story?
3 Why was Rosaura invited to the party?
4 What impression do you get of other children at the party?
5 What impression do you get of Senora Ines?
6 The story ends with both Senora Ines and Rosaura refusing to move. What do you think happened in the end?

Writing

When they get home, Rosaura and her mother talk about what happened. Write their conversation.

Harrison Bergeron

Discussion

1 What was the point of the handicapping and how was it supposed to work?
2 What is the author making fun of in this story?
3 Do you agree with him? What are your reasons?
4 Would it be a good thing to have a society in which all people were really equal?
5 Would it be possible?

Writing

Choose one of these topics to write about.

1 Your thoughts and opinions about the story and what the author is saying in it.
2 You are the Handicapper General. Make up a set of rules to guide your Assistant Handicappers.
3 Think about what life would be like in school in this society. Write an account of a day at school in 2081 when 'everybody was finally equal'.

After you, my dear Alphonse

Writing

Write the following short conversations:

1) Between Johnny and Boyd, about parents.
2) Between Boyd and his parents about Johnny and Mrs Wilson.
3) Between Mrs Wilson and her husband about Boyd's visit.

The Qualification and Girls can we educate we Dads?

Both these poems are written in dialect. At first sight you may find them difficult to follow. If so, try reading them aloud. Work out what the dialect is and try to make the poems sound right.

Discussion and comment

1 What is the theme of each poem?
2 Do you agree with what each poet is saying?
3 What is the effect of the use of dialect in each case?

Men talk

Group reading

This poem was written to be performed. Work on a group reading of it:

1 Each member of the group reads the poem to him/herself.
2 The group discusses the poem and how it should be performed.
3 The poem is divided up into sections for reading by:
    one voice
    two voices together
    the whole group in chorus.
    (You can even have two voices reading different parts at the same time.)
4 The parts are given out.
5 The group practises reading the poem.

Interlude: St George

1 The city of Sylene is terrorised by the dragon.

2 The citizens feed it sheep to keep it happy

5 The King's daughter draws the unlucky lot.

6 She is sacrificed to the dragon.

9 He leads it into the city. People are terrified.

10 He promises the citizens if they become Christians . . .

the dragon has eaten the last sheep . . .

4 . . . the citizens decide to draw lots to see who will be fed to the dragon next.

orge comes to the rescue.

8 He harnesses the dragon with the princess's silk girdle.

will kill the dragon.

12 He gives his reward to the poor.

St George and the dragons

It had all the signs of a good dragon. Burning farms, stricken villages, fleeing peasants. This would be his forty-seventh; but he still got that good old tight feeling of excitement in his belly. He headed where the columns of rising smoke were thickest. His horse quickened its stride, sniffing the sooty air with gusto.

The helpless maiden was exactly where he thought she'd be; after all these years he could find the lady pretty quickly. She was tied by the usual cruel bonds to the usual gnarled oak. Naked, of course, but the dragon had arranged her long red hair with discretion. Good to be dealing with a dragon that knew its business...

Which was more than the maiden did, apparently. Instead of piteous wails, she was silent. Far from tears of joy at the sight of him, she glowered. A good-looking lady, but a powerful chin. A girl to rescue, but not to dally with.

'Stop ogling me like I was on Page Three!'

'Madam,' he said, shocked.

'And don't just sit there saying "Madam" from a great height? Your sort make me sick. You're deliberately keeping me from my clothes, like all oppressors do, to destroy their victim's sense of personal identity. How'd you like to keep your end up, socially, naked and immobilised? Apparently you need to cover *your* shrunken ego with boiler-plate, before you can pretend to relate to anybody...'

'I'm wearing armour because I've got a job to do.'

'You mean you weren't wearing it before you saw the smoke-columns? You mean you got *changed* before you galloped to my rescue? From the look of you, you *sleep* in the damn stuff.

'And that twelve-foot lance. Kill at a distance, huh? Never feel the dragon as a living thing, a beating heart? Never feel its throat gasping for breath under your hands? Never get dirty with its spurting blood? Too real for yah? Cut me loose and gimme my clothes.'

He dismounted, profoundly wishing he was elsewhere. It was difficult to cut her loose without looking at her. Worse, she did not dress immediately, but stood weighing him up.

'You're not a bad-looking guy, what I can see of yah. How's about taking off your armour? I never got acquainted with a real reactionary chauvinist knight. But I'm broadminded...'

'Madam, I have work to do!'

She sighed. Then said derisively 'Make love not war'. Then added 'Where d'you think *you're* off to?'

'I have a dragon to kill.'

'Just like, that, huh? Don't bother to ask yourself whether it's a good dragon or a bad dragon? Whether it's got a wife and kids at home? Whether it's supporting aged parents, or a handicapped sibling? Just kill it, huh?'

'You've seen the burning farms, the stricken villages, the fleeing peasants...'

'Ever consider things from the dragon's viewpoint? Maybe all this land belonged to the dragon in the first place? Maybe the peasants robbed it, with their commercial exploitation of Planet Earth? Maybe this land is sacred to dragon-culture? Ever talk to any of the dragons you kill, before you kill them?'

'Madam, the dragons approach with searing flame. Unless you get in an accurate first blow....'

'They turn you into a pot-roast, huh?' She laughed, nastily, pulling on a pair of uncomely vertical-striped breeches, held up by long straps across her shoulders. 'It's tragic, really. You guys are brought up by so-called loving parents, who teach you that dragons are only for killing. And the dragons are brought up by so-called loving parents and taught that knights are only for roasting. You're both the helpless victims of your own death-centred cultures...'

'I must leave you. The dragon is approaching.' Suddenly, St George knew where he was again. This dragon was a full-grown beast, in good shape. It had several old lance-wounds in its neck; small feeble wounds. It must have killed several knights. It tested its fiery breath, when it was still a hundred yards away. Grass seared like a sudden autumn; several small trees burst into flame. But it seemed to have difficulty swinging its long neck to the right. Attack from the right and behind, then. It did not look too quick on its feet. A feint at its left shoulder, a last-minute swerve...

'Hold it, buster,' said the maiden. 'It'll talk to *me*. I've spent a few hours relating to it. Eye-to-eye contact. It sees me as a fellow living being, a fellow-inhabitant of the planet. It wants a closer relationship with me . . . a continuing open-ended relationship . . .'

'Madam, it will *devour* you!'

'That's your blind conditioning talking. Actually, it's made me rather an interesting proposal; for a dragon. Put up your lance, buster. It's *my* dragon.'

St George could only watch helplessly. She walked straight up to it. Established eye-to-eye contact. Put a shapely white arm round its scaly neck, and talked. And talked. And talked. Jaw, jaw, he thought sadly, not war, war.

Finally, arm still round its neck, she brought it over. The dragon gave St George a rather contemptuous nod. 'You don't have to die today, buster. I know you're just a guy trying to do his job. An unwilling victim of the violent society you live in. Make love, not war. This day starts a new era in human-dragon relationships. And remember it was we dragons made the first move. Go beat your sword into a plough-share. Have a nice day . . .'

The maiden put both slender white arms lovingly round the dragon's scaly neck and said to St George 'You had your chance with me, buster. You can't complain.'

The only thing St George could do was ride away.

*   *   *

He came across the dragon again, three months later. It was ambling aimlessly, head down. Didn't even see him as he came thundering up, lance at the ready.

He couldn't take advantage. He backed off some yards, and issued a formal challenge.

The dragon raised a listless head. Its once-brilliant faceted eyes were as dull as dish cloths. The sharp spines all along its back drooped. Its hide was floppy and wrinkled, and the scales were falling off. It looked as docile as a cow.

It did draw itself up for a fiery blast from its mouth . . .

'No good, huh?' it asked afterwards.

'I felt a certain warmth on my face,' said St George charitably. He felt great pity for the beast.

'She got me eating *grass*. I'm deficient in calcium, protein, sulphur . . . that's what's done for my fiery breath.'

'Where is she?' asked St George nervously.

'Got herself a new dragon. Said she'd done all she could for me, and it was better this way. I'd be grateful if you'd kill me now. I keep getting bitten by dogs. There's no future. I want the hell out.'

'I'm into combat,' said St George. 'Not euthanasia . . .'

'I could attack you . . .'

'No,' said St George with a shudder. He couldn't face the feel of that bovine grass-laden breath in his face again. And the creature's hind legs had sat down of their own accord, like the back end of a pantomime horse, without its noticing.

'Take me round with you, until I get fit again. Even a few dead rabbits would help. Then I could give you a decent match. If I go on like this I'm scared I'll lie down and get eaten by *ants*. I never minded dying on the lance of a good knight. That way I'll go where good dragons go . . .'

'I haven't the time,' said St George regretfully. 'There are other dragons to slay . . .'

The dragon shook its head lugubriously. 'There ain't. Them maidens have got something going among themselves. There's a whole Maidens' Movement . . .'

St George believed him. The dragon was too heart-sick to lie.

*   *   *   *   *

Three months later, the dragon pronounced himself fit.

'Like a bit of fun, first?' asked St George. 'Bit of pillaging, burning? A last spree?'

'That'd be pushing my luck,' said the dragon. 'Might meet a maiden again.'

He made a good fight of it. When the final lance-thrust went home, and the dragon body began to self-combust, the way all dragon bodies should, St George watched the magic green smoke drifting across the plain, and knew the dragon had gone where good dragons should go.

He was so lost in thankful thought that he hardly felt the gentle nudge at his shoulder. He spun round.

Two more woebegone dragons stood there.

'Are you St George?' asked the first one, weakly. 'A friend of ours told us you might be able to help . . .'

'All right,' said St George wearily. His heart was heavy at the prospect; but after all, he was supposed to be a saint.

Slowly they wound away over the desolate plain.

None of them was ever seen again.

Robert Westall

St George and the dragon
by Ucello, National Gallery, London

Not my best side

I

Not my best side, I'm afraid.
The artist didn't give me a chance to
Pose properly, and as you can see,
Poor chap, he had this obsession with
Triangles, so he left off two of my
Feet. I didn't comment at the time
(What, after all, are two feet
To a monster?) but afterwards
I was sorry for the bad publicity.
Why, I said to myself, should my conqueror
Be so ostentatiously beardless, and ride
A horse with a deformed neck and square hoofs?
Why should my victim be so
Unattractive as to be inedible,
And why should she have me literally
On a string? I don't mind dying
Ritually, since I always rise again,
But I should have liked a little more blood
To show they were taking me seriously.

II

It's hard for a girl to be sure if
She wants to be rescued. I mean, I quite
Took to the dragon. It's nice to be
Liked, if you know what I mean. He was
So nicely physical, with his claws
And lovely green skin, and that sexy tail,
And the way he looked at me,
He made me feel he was all ready to
Eat me. And any girl enjoys that.
So when this boy turned up, wearing machinery,
On a really *dangerous* horse, to be honest,
I didn't much fancy him. I mean,
What was he like underneath the hardware?
He might have acne, blackheads or even
Bad breath for all I could tell, but the dragon –
Well, you could see all his equipment
At a glance. Still, what could I do?
The dragon got himself beaten by the boy,
And a girl's got to think of her future.

III

I have diplomas in Dragon
Management and Virgin Reclamation.
My horse is the latest model, with
Automatic transmission and built-in
Obsolescence. My spear is custom-built,
And my prototype armour
Still on the secret list. You can't
Do better than me at the moment.
I'm qualified and equipped to the
Eyebrow. So why be difficult?
Don't you want to be killed and/or rescued
In the most contemporary way? Don't
You want to carry out the roles
That sociology and myth have designed for you?
Don't you realise that, by being choosy,
You are endangering job-prospects
In the spear- and horse-building industries?
What, in any case, does it matter what
You want? You're in my way.

U.A. Fanthorpe

Activities

St George

Tell this story in two different ways. Choose from this list.

1 So that it could be understood and enjoyed by a child of junior school age.
2 As a radio news item.
3 As told by the General Secretary of the National Union of Dragons.
4 As told by a member of the local Dragon Hunting Association.

St George and the Dragons

Discussion

Robert Westall has used a well-known story to put across a number of his own ideas.

1 How would you sum up those ideas?
2 How many of them do you share and why?
3 Why do you think he chose the story of St George?
4 What is your opinion of treating traditional stories in this way?

Not my best side

Questions

This poem is based on the picture on page 144. Study both carefully, and see how the writer has made use of the painting. Make notes on the following questions.

1 The poem is in three sections. What is each one about?
2 What does the dragon think of the painting and why?
3 How does he think he should have been painted?
4 What does the girl think of:
   a) the dragon?
   b) St George?
5 What is the meaning of the last line of section 2?
6 What does St George think of himself?

Writing

Look at the answers you have given to the questions. Think about how the writer has used the story and the picture. Now write about the poem and its message.

Generations

Partly because

Partly because of the mistakes I made
I felt obliged to say to my son
be kind to people
be a kind seller of seeds
or petrol-pump attendant instead of an unkind lawyer
or an uncaring director of personnel.

I could only say it once
and he has gone away
chasing butterflies
but what he does to them
if they are caught
if they are in his power
I am never there to see.

Ursula Laird

148

Saturday song

He was about fourteen, clean, tidy and unlovely. Some sort of skin complaint, he was told; you'll grow out of it soon, he was promised. Meanwhile, he kept his boiled-looking face as much to himself as possible, and when he rubbed and scratched the raw cracks in his hands under his school desk, the teacher asked him what he was fidgeting with, and the other boys sniggered. Apart from scratching his hands, he seldom made any superfluous movements. So he was not kicking stones or crushing handfuls of the dusty hedge on that bright October morning. He just sat quietly on a low wall, clutching a small case and a cheap plastic folder under his arm. The wall faced the back of a row of crumbling houses, and the boy was staring absently at a broken window in the second house from the end.

An old man came slowly along the lane and into the yard. When he saw the boy, he stiffened, straightened his back and gathered his bulging string shopping bags close to him.

'What do you want?' He sounded weary. There was no answer. 'I said, what d'you want?' There was fear in the old man's voice.

There was a pause, then the boy said, 'Nothing. I'm just waiting.'

'Well you can't wait here. On your way, laddie!'

'No. I'll just stay. It's too early to go yet. I won't get in your way.' The boy spoke politely.

The old man almost mustered a roar, 'Move, son! I suppose it was your lot done that! Just get out of here and leave me in peace. Away home and break your own windows!'

'I'm sorry about your window,' said the boy, 'but I've just got here.' He stood up.

'I'm only waiting for a while, but I'll move along there if you like.'

He turned towards the old man, towards the other end of the shabby terrace, his mild blue eyes blinking and watering in the sun. There was no menace in him after all, no anger, except in the red blotchy skin. The old man sagged, too tired to argue any more. He handed over his bags and his keys as if to a neighbour of long standing. 'Will you carry the messages in for me, lad? They're heavier than I thought.'

The door opened into a narrow, stone-floored hallway smelly with paraffin cans, old newspapers and the passing attentions of cats. The boy had to squeeze himself against flaking, grey distemper to let the old man pass him and open the door half-way along the hall. A new set of smells and the twittering of a budgie greeted them as they entered the living-room.

The boy almost retched as the combined odours of birdcage, bed and old age reached him. The old man, unnoticing, said, 'Come in, son. This is where I live. It's not very grand, but it does me fine. Could you put some coal on? It's a bit cold.'

He sank into a worn, lumpy armchair. The boy put the string bags on the table and laid down his own case and folder too. He looked around for tongs or a shovel, then used his hands, reluctantly.

'Who's C.P.M.?'

The boy turned, startled. The old man was looking at the case. 'Oh, that was my Dad, Colin Peter Morrison. I'm just Peter.'

'Your Dad's passed on, then? What's in the case?'

'Nothing. A clarinet. It was my Dad's.'

The old man looked eager. 'Can you play it?'

'No!'

'Not even a wee bit?'

'No. I hate it!'

'Are you learning to play it?'

'No. My Mum sent me to lessons. But I hate it. Can I wash my hands?'

'Over there. Why d'you hate it?'

But Peter turned on the tap and washed his hands carefully. Then since the water was hot, he wiped out the greasy sink and started to wash the dishes which were in the sink, beside the sink, on the table and on the mantelpiece. He wet an old cloth which was bundled on the wooden draining-board, and washed off the ash and coal-dust and tea stains from the hearth. He looked at the filthy cloth.

'I think I should just throw this away now.'

'Aye! You're a tidy fellow. D'you like the bird? Her name's Jinty. She's good company.'

'Uh-huh. My Dad used to keep birds, but my Mum never liked them. I could clean out the cage. Does she get out?'

'She'll not go far. She likes the mantelpiece.'

Peter opened the cage door with the bird trying to peck his fingers. It fluttered on to the old man's head, flew over to one of the square, varnished

bedposts and finally settled on the brightly-painted toffee-tin above the fireplace, squawking quietly.

The old man said soothingly, 'Sssh, beauty, sssh! He's just making your house nice. He'll not hurt you.'

Peter crossed to the sink to fill the little water bowl. 'Where d'you keep the birdseed?'

'Here, I've just bought some more. She'll soon get used to you.' He hesitated, then added, 'She'll know you next time.'

'Mr Briggs, could I . . . ?'

'How d'you know my name?' the old man asked sharply.

'Your pension book. It's on the mantelpiece. It's just a different colour from my Mum's.'

'Don't miss much, do you, son?' he mumbled.

'Mr Briggs, I could come for a while on Saturdays, and . . . and help you. You know, clean up a bit, or go to the shops. I haven't . . . I mean, there's nothing else to do.' Peter held his finger out to the budgie. The bird ignored him, flew back to the cage and warbled at its reflection in the tiny mirror. 'Would you like me to wash the window? I've still got time.'

'Leave it, lad. You can do it next week.'

Peter shut the door of the birdcage. 'Oh! Fine! I'll come about ten.'

'That'll be nice.' The old man's gaze was resting on the clarinet case. 'Why d'you hate it?'

'What? Oh! I just do.'

'Play us a tune.'

'No! I've told you! I can't. I'll need to go now.' The red patches glowed on Peter's face and neck.

'What were you waiting for, son?'

'Nothing. It doesn't matter.' Behind his back he rubbed his itching hands against his trousers, against each other. 'Will I come next Saturday then?'

He tucked the clarinet and the folder under his arm. The old man was running his thumb-nail back and forward over the top of the birdcage. 'What d'you think, Jinty? Will we let him come back? Maybe he'll give us a tune next time.'

The bird cocked its head, first to one side, then to the other. Peter opened the door into the damp hallway.

'Jinty says you can come. You could wait at the end of the lane and carry the messages. If you want to.'

Peter's fiery skin began to cool. 'Right! Cheerio! See you on Saturday, Mr Briggs.'

'Shut the doors behind you, son!'

Peter shut the living-room door. Going down the hall, he added shyly, 'Cheerio, Jinty.'

Their Saturday mornings settled into an easy routine. Peter, always with the clarinet and music-folder under his arm, would meet Mr Briggs outside the corner shop. The old man would hand over his bags and they would walk slowly, companionably, along the lane which became barer and muddier as the weeks went on. Once inside the house, the boy would fill the coal buckets while the old man made tea. They would drink it in front of the fire and slip cake crumbs to the budgie through the bars of the cage. Then Peter would gather up everything that looked like rubbish, take it out to the dustbin and push an ancient, rattling sweeper over the thin carpet. He would clean out the birdcage, and wash the window, if it wasn't raining. Mr Briggs would potter around, put away his meagre groceries, start to peel potatoes, then abandon them in favour of another mug of stewed tea.

The conversation was hardly more varied than the housework.

'And how's the school, lad?'

'Fine.'

'Doing all right then?'

'Uh-huh.'

'You mind and stick in. I wish I had.'

'Uh-huh.'

Peter would brace himself for the next bit.

'How about a wee tune, then? Me and Jinty would like a wee tune. Wouldn't we, beauty?' The bird would trill obligingly.

Sometimes the old man held out the clarinet case towards the boy. Sometimes he would open it and stroke the red plush lining, or run his finger along the dark, shiny wood. 'C' mon son. Play us a tune.'

'No! I can't.'

'Aw, you could if you tried.'

'I don't want to!'

Mr Briggs would shake his head, sigh loudly and return to his potato peeling, looking hurt. Eventually he would say, 'Is there time for more tea?'

And Peter would look at his watch, pick up his things and say, 'No. I'd better be going. Will I come again next week?'

They would both look round the hot, tidy room.

'Aye, laddie. See you next Saturday.'

The last Saturday in November was wild and stormy. Peter was already soaked by the time Mr Briggs came out of the shop with his usual string bags tucked inside plastic carriers. They ploughed along the filthy lane, heads down against the rain, bumping into each other as they fought the wind. The old man kept tugging at his hat and pulling up his coat collar, but Peter had the shopping in one hand and the clarinet and music-case in the other, and the rain dribbled unchecked round his neck and wrists.

'It's a dirty day, all right,' said Mr Briggs, sounding quite cheerful. 'I wondered if you'd bother coming.'

'I said I would.' The carrier-bags cut into Peter's hand, and he thought he might drop something.

'You're a good lad. We'll soon be home. The fire should be just nice when we get in.'

They turned into the yard and the wind blew the bags against Peter's wet legs as he struggled across the path to the door. When the door was opened, Peter almost fell into the hallway. He hurried into the stuffy, fetid living-room and dropped everything in a heap on the table. His hands were aching with cold, and he stood about miserably while Mr Briggs hung up his coat and hat, and filled the kettle.

'Get that wet jacket off you, son. You'll maybe have to stay a bit longer, till it dries. I'll make the tea. You sit and warm yourself.'

Peter took off his anorak and bundled it over the back of a chair. The old man had poked the fire and put pieces of coal round it without spoiling its blazing heart. Peter held out his hands to it, knowing that he should have rubbed his dripping hair and patted the wet cracks between his fingers.

Already he could feel his face becoming taut in the dry heat. He crossed to the sink, let the water run for a minute, then put the stopper in. 'I'd better get busy. There's a lot to do.'

Mr Briggs reached from behind him and turned off the tap. 'Nothing that won't wait, laddie. Come away from there. Just sit down, like I said, and get this tea inside you.'

Peter sat in one of the fireside chairs with his hands wrapped round the steaming mug. Mr Briggs brought a plate of sticky buns and put it on the hearth near the boy.

'Mind and save some bits for Jinty. I'll let her out for a wee flutter.' He opened the cage, but the bird remained on its perch, singing ecstatically. He looked at the budgie fondly.

'She likes when it's raining. She knows fine we'll not rush off and leave her.'

He held out a piece of his bun into the cage. The bird pecked it out of his fingers, dropped it and went on singing. 'Cheeky thing!' he said indulgently.

Peter started to drink his tea. His face was burning, and between mouthfuls of tea and bun he hunched up first one shoulder, then the other, and rubbed the flaming patches on his cheeks against his rough sweater.

'What's wrong lad?'

'Nothing.'

'You don't look right. What's wrong with your face?'

'Nothing!'

Before the old man could ask any more questions, the bird flew out of the cage and rested for a moment on Peter's head on its way to the mantelpiece. The old man was delighted. 'Oh, I knew she'd get used to you! She likes you! You'll not get rid of her next week!'

'I won't be here next week,' said Peter quietly.

'What? Why not?'

'I can't come. I won't be coming again. I'll just tidy up a bit now. Maybe during the holidays . . .,' he said half-heartedly, while rubbing his itching hands on his trousers. He brought the carpet-sweeper out from the cupboard in the wall and pushed it around the middle of the room. Mr Briggs kept getting in the way.

'Why can't you come? Why did you come in the first place?'

'It doesn't matter.'

Peter left the sweeper standing, took a duster from under the sink and swept it smartly along the mantelpiece. The startled bird swooped round the room three times before heading for the cage. Peter's hand reached the cage door first.

'No you don't! I'm going to clean your cage properly – and you keep it clean!'

The bird sat on top of the cage looking puzzled.

'Just leave it, son. She's tired. Leave it till next week.'

'I told you! I won't be back!'

'You haven't told me much. Why are you here?'

Peter ignored him. 'I'll just give her clean water,' he said, taking the plastic bowl to the tap. The bird scrambled into the cage, and the boy replaced the bowl and shut the door.

'You should be up at the school, shouldn't you?' The old man was jubilant

154

when he saw the change in Peter's face. 'Shouldn't you?'

'No!'

'I heard about those music lessons. Trumpets and flutes and violins. All sorts of things. And clarinets!' he added triumphantly.

'I don't have to go!'

'Aye, but that's where your Ma thinks you've gone! Isn't it?' He lifted the clarinet case from the table and thrust it under Peter's nose. The boy turned his head away.

'What happened son? Why can't you come next week? Did someone tell on you?'

'No! But I can't come back.'

Peter busied himself at the sink. He thought of all the excuses he had already given his music teacher. He thought of all the other excuses he had stored up ready, but which he could not now use because his music teacher had stopped believing him. At least he could blame the weather this week. He heard Mr Briggs opening the catches of the case and waited for the dreaded wheedling words.

'We'll surely get a tune this time, Jinty. He couldn't leave us without a tune!'

Peter clashed the dishes in the soapy water. He pulled out the stopper and piled them on the draining-board.

'C'mon son. You know how much we want to hear you play! We don't mind if you're not very good!'

Peter half-dried his sore, raw hands. He took his anorak from the chair near the fire and put it on. It steamed with his body's heat. He started to tidy the bags he had dumped on the table, first laying his music-folder on one side.

'Maybe he can't play at all, Jinty! Maybe he just carries that case because it looks nice! If he doesn't play us a tune this time, we'll never know, will we?'

The itch between Peter's fingers was unbearable. He rushed the sweeper across the room and jammed it into a corner. 'All right! All right!'

He snatched the case from the old man's hands and banged it down on the table. Deftly, he screwed the sections of the clarinet together, lining up the keys as if it was the habit of a lifetime. He took the protective metal cap off the mouthpiece, sucked the reed before positioning it and tightened the silver ligature which kept it in place. Mr Briggs was fascinated by the busy, skilful hands. He only noticed the boy's grim face when it glared redly a few inches from his own. He shrank back into his armchair.

Peter hissed at him. 'I'll give you a tune! And your stupid bird as well! You've asked for it. You'll be sorry. Here's a tune for you!'

He stuck the clarinet angrily in his mouth and blasted hard, crude notes at the old man, repeating the vulgar theme over and over like a cruel, taunting child.

Hands to his ears, Mr Briggs whimpered, 'Stop it! Oh, stop it, lad! It doesn't matter about the tune. You're frightening the bird!'

The terrified budgie was screeching and flapping, banging itself off the sides of the cage, scattering birdseed and water and tiny green feathers through the bars. Peter turned away from the old man. He blew long, unpitched rasps towards the bird, holding the clarinet in one hand while he opened the cage door with the other. He pushed the bell of the instrument into the cage, crouching level with the table on which it stood. The little quivering creature scrambled dementedly between floor and perch. It puffed out its heaving breast as if to push away the vicious, insistent tune. Mr Briggs stumbled over from his chair and pummelled Peter with his old soft fists, pleading and sobbing.

The bird was suddenly calm. It chirped once, and keeled over on its side at the bottom of the cage, one tiny eye staring beadily upwards. It gave a gentle shudder, then lay still. Peter stared in horror at the dead bird.

The old man wailed, 'You've killed her! You wee bugger! You wicked wee bugger! You've killed Jinty! Oh, the poor bird! You've killed her!'

The boy pulled the clarinet roughly out of the cage and ran out of the room and down the hallway, with the cries ringing in his ears. He ran across the yard and along the lane, ran all the way home in the driving, sleety rain. At last he stood, dripping and panting, on his doorstep and fumbled for his key. At some point he must have put the instrument inside his anorak for protection, and he realised, as his fingers touched the clammy wood, that he had left the clarinet-case behind.

The wind had died and the rain was a fine drizzle when Peter went back to the house after school on Monday. He crossed the muddy yard and was relieved to find the front door unlocked and swinging slightly in the breeze. Rain had blown into the hallway. There was no rush of warmth from the living-room as he opened the door. The fire was out, a heap of fine ash spilling over on to the hearth, and the usual smells were suspended in the chill air.

The birdcage was shrouded in its flowered night-time cover. Mr Briggs lay back in his armchair, his legs stretched stiffly in front of him, his mouth open. Peter was surprised that he was not snoring. He called his name softly. Then, since there was no answer, he tiptoed to the cluttered table and gathered up his case and his music-folder. 'Cheerio, Mr Briggs,' he said quietly. He left the cold, silent house, shutting the door behind him.

After his tea he went upstairs to his bedroom. He assembled the instrument and propped up 'Daily Exercises for the Clarinet Student' on the bookshelf. He started to practise. A family of starlings chattered and complained outside his window. Before long his eyes were filled with tears and he had to stop to blow his nose. He started playing again. The third time the music came to a sort of gurgling halt, his mother wondered downstairs if perhaps the clarinet lessons were a waste of time.

Maureen Monaghan

The animal house

I have a lion, a furry faced lion.
He dominantly controls the household.
He eats a lot of meat and he snarls if I pester him.
He is out most of the day. I call him dad.

I also have a dove.
She works all day too, but she works at home,
She is soft, gentle, kind and cares for her young,
She is always there if I need her, I call her mum.

I have a peacock.
She has a head with lots of different colours.
She has green eyes and a beautiful coat.
She has a tuft of glittery hair at the front, I call her my punk sister.

I have a kitten.
He is so small and smooth.
He has teeny little eyes and a wet nose.
He drinks milk a lot, and cries a lot, I call him baby brother.

Then there's me,
I know what I am.
I'm the black sheep.

Sandy Brechin

The signature

The day my mother cried because she could not sign her name, I vowed to teach her, not only to sign Vashti Deen on government forms and my school reports, but also to read and write as well as I, an eighth-grader of no little accomplishment.

In all my thirteen years nothing distressed me more than my mother's tears that day over a failure that was not of her making. Her grandparents, like my father's, had been conscripted for the British colonial sugar armies in 1845, and my parents were there in Trinidad, near Venezuela, one hundred and ten years later, still fighting to master the English language and its different world.

My mother had gone up to the Warden's Office in nearby Camdentown to get my elder sister's birth certificate, and, as far as I could gather, had been kept waiting in a queue for 'illiterates'. Then, when her turn came to be served, she had made the mistake of writing her X mark in the wrong place on the request form. A recently educated clerk had abused her needlessly. He called her 'an ignorant coolie'. This was far removed from the truth. Though she could not write, my mother spoke Bengali and knew the ancient Indian world scriptures. She used to recite poetry to us, and while we did not understand the language she spoke, the sound of it was of the most delicate and persuasive beauty.

My mother did not think that the old language would help her children survive in the new ways of the modern world. She knew that she had to choose the road to modernisation and in us had given up the old ways for everything English, which was the way of life.

By the end of the Second World War some cane-cutters of my parents' generation had attended schools in which English was taught. But my parents were among the thousands who never made it to these schools. Having been too deeply steeped in the ways of the old country, Ma and Pa stuck to their Hindu life.

Well, when my mother came home crying that day we were all upset. She gave no immediate reason for her tears. She went to her bedroom and we hoped that, as was the custom, she would favour us with an explanation. My father tied the cow under the mango tree at the back of our mud house. My sisters looked at me and at each other and went on cooking chapatis over the coalpot.

The next day we heard the story from our father; it was then I volunteered to undertake my mother's English education.

For the next few days, whenever she could spare time away from her work in the cane fields and in our home, she would sit at the kitchen table and repeat the alphabet after me:

'A, B, C, D, ...' She would get to G and forget, would adjust her *orhani* head-covering impatiently and try again.

In a few weeks Ma learned the alphabet. She wanted to go on to sentences. I tried to follow my teacher's approach: 'the simplest first' was Mr Joefield's motto. I even copied his patient manner and, unconsciously, his accent.

'We have to try spelling first, Ma,' I cautioned, 'then we can do sentences.'

Sometimes my sisters would try to help but, as they had left school as soon as their breasts appeared ('Women are supposed to be at home,' was my father's edict), they were of little help, not knowing anything of case, tense, mood and all those advanced things with which I was familiar in the eighth grade.

My father laughed at this family schooling effort, but Ma was not put off; and neither was I.

Six months after we began Ma became quite skilled at writing her name down, in a spidery sort of way, but her signature nonetheless. She had practised for hours that gesture of worth until it was mastered. I recall her sitting at the kitchen table in her cane-ash-covered cotton skirt and shirt tails tied at the front, practising, practising, practising; dipping the nib tied to the hibiscus stalk into the Quink ink bottle.

'Ma,' I said one day, 'you don't have to treat me like if I doing you a favour. Is my duty to teach you.'

You see, I was feeling badly about the extra things she would do for me now; tie the cow out for me before she went to work. Or rush home to make me my favourite *mohanbhoag* pudding.

'Gwan boy,' she replied, 'you must keep all your strength for school. You have to study hard. And one day you go have a education. And you not going to have to work like me and your Pa. Labouring is no joke, boy. You go see. When you get big you go see.'

Now that I tell the story I remember that whenever my mother sat down to practise her signature her face became almost angelic. It lit up with a kind of softness; concentration and pride I suppose. She tried to sign her name like an old hand at it, effortlessly, and after a while she did, although her fingers were always smeared with ink. She would go outside to the rainwater barrel to wash it off and start all over again. Practising her signature and counting became an obsession.

After a while my father stopped being amused at her efforts. And Ma continued to progress. She no longer called money 'cent', but stated precise amounts when paying the fisherman and the shopkeeper. Her new-found arithmetic skills astonished them.

She began reading my old First Primer:
'Sam and Pam like jam. Tim and Tot like ham.'
'Can a pig dance a jig for a fig?'

But my mother never put her signature on a government form or my school report. It was six in the morning that day when my father woke me. 'Your mother dead, boy,' he said.

A cane stalk had pierced her heel in the fields at Watergut, about five miles up the road from our house. She had gone out long before dawn to complete her 'task', as a cutter's yardage of cane was called. She was working alone when the cane stalk penetrated her heel. A trail of blood told that she had tried to make her way back to the road; but she bled to death. No one had heard her. I heard the story repeated to the barber, the estate foreman, the Negro neighbour, my aunts and uncles, to everyone who came weeping to our house.

Until the following day, the day of the cremation, I wandered about our village clutching the piece of brown shopping-bag paper my mother had left on the kitchen table before she had gone to the fields.

I still keep it in my wallet today, even though so many years have passed and I am exiled to a far country. I unfold that square of paper many times. I see the inkstained, childish hand: Vashti Deen.

Clyde Hosein

To hell with dying

'To hell with dying,' my father would say. 'These children want Mr Sweet!'

Mr Sweet was a diabetic and an alcoholic and a guitar player and lived down the road from us on a neglected cotton farm. My older brothers and sisters got the most benefit from Mr Sweet, for when they were growing up he had quite a few years ahead of him and so was capable of being called back from the brink of death any number of times – whenever the voice of my father reached him as he lay expiring. 'To hell with dying, man,' my father would say, pushing the wife away from the bedside (in tears although she knew the death was not necessarily the last one unless Mr Sweet really wanted it to be). 'These children want Mr Sweet!' And they did want him, for at a signal from Father they would come crowding around the bed and throw themselves on the covers, and whoever was the smallest at the time would kiss him all over his wrinkled brown face and begin to tickle him so that he would laugh all down in his stomach, and his moustache, which was long and sort of straggly, would shake like Spanish moss and was also that colour.

Mr Sweet had been ambitious as a boy, wanted to be a doctor or lawyer or sailor, only to find that black men fare better if they are not. Since he could become none of these things he turned to fishing as his only earnest career and playing the guitar as his only claim to doing anything extraordinarily well. His son, the only one that he and his wife, Miss Mary, had, was shiftless as the day is long and spent money as if he were trying to see the bottom of the mint, which Mr Sweet would tell him was the clean brown palm of his hand. Miss Mary loved her 'baby', however, and worked hard to get him the 'li'l necessaries' of life, which turned out mostly to be women.

Mr Sweet was a tall, thinnish man with thick kinky hair going dead white. He was dark brown, his eyes were very squinty and sort of bluish, and he chewed Brown Mule tobacco. He was constantly on the verge of being blind drunk, for he brewed his own liquor and was not in the least a stingy sort of man, and was always very melancholy and sad, though frequently when he was 'feelin' good' he'd dance around the yard with us, usually keeling over just as my mother came to see what the commotion was.

Toward all of us children he was very kind, and had the grace to be shy with us, which is unusual in grown-ups. He had great respect for my mother for she never held his drunkenness against him and would let us play with him even when he was about to fall in the fireplace from drink. Although Mr Sweet would sometimes lose complete or nearly complete control of his head and neck so that he would loll in his chair, his mind remained strangely acute and his speech not too affected. His ability to be drunk and sober at the same time made him an ideal playmate, for he was as weak as we were and we could usually best him in wrestling, all the while keeping a fairly coherent conversation going.

We never felt anything of Mr Sweet's age when we played with him. We loved his wrinkles and would draw some on our brows to be like him, and his white hair was my special treasure and he knew it and would never come to visit us just after he had had his hair cut off at the barbershop. Once he came to our house for something, probably to see my father about fertiliser for his crops because, although he never paid the slightest attention to his crops, he liked to know what things would be best to use on them if he ever did. Anyhow, he had not come with his hair since he had just had it shaved off at the barbershop. He wore a huge straw hat to keep off the sun and also to keep his head away from me. But as soon as I saw him I ran up and demanded that he take me up and kiss me with his funny beard which smelled so strongly of tobacco. Looking forward to burying my small fingers into his woolly hair I threw away his hat only to find he had done something to his hair, that it was no longer there! I let out a squall which made my mother think that Mr Sweet had finally dropped me in the well or something and from that day I've been wary of men in hats. However, not long after, Mr Sweet showed up with his hair grown out and just as white and kinky and impenetrable as it ever was.

Mr Sweet used to call me his princess, and I believed it. He made me feel pretty at five and six, and simply outrageously devastating at the blazing age of eight and a half. When he came to our house with his guitar the whole family would stop whatever they were doing to sit around him and listen to him play. He liked to play 'Sweet Georgia Brown', that was what he called me sometimes, and also he liked to play 'Caldonia' and all sorts of sweet, sad, wonderful songs which he sometimes made up. It was from one of these songs that I learned that he had had to marry Miss Mary when he had in fact loved somebody else (now living in Chi-ca-go, or De-stroy, Michigan). He was not sure that Joe Lee, her 'baby', was also his baby. Sometimes he would cry and that was an indication that he was about to die again. And so we would all get prepared, for we were sure to be called upon.

I was seven the first time I remember actually participating in one of Mr Sweet's 'revivals' – my parents told me I had participated before, I had been the one chosen to kiss him and tickle him long before I knew the rite of Mr

Sweet's rehabilitation. He had come to our house, it was a few years after his wife's death, and was very sad, and also, typically, very drunk. He sat on the floor next to me and my older brother, the rest of the children were grown up and lived elsewhere, and began to play his guitar and cry. I held his woolly head in my arms and wished I could have been old enough to have been the woman he loved so much and that I had not been lost years and years ago.

When he was leaving, my mother said to us that we'd better sleep light that night for we'd probably have to go over to Mr Sweet's before daylight. And we did. For soon after we had gone to bed one of the neighbours knocked on our door and called my father and said that Mr Sweet was sinking fast and if he wanted to get in a word before the crossover he'd better shake a leg and get over to Mr Sweet's house. All the neighbours knew to come to our house if something was wrong with Mr Sweet, but they did not know how we always managed to make him well, or at least stop him from dying, when he was often so near death. As soon as we heard the cry we got up, my brother and I and my mother and father, and put on our clothes. We hurried out of the house and down the road for we were always afraid that we might someday be too late and Mr Sweet would get tired of dallying.

When we got to the house, a very poor shack really, we found the front room full of neighbours and relatives and someone met us at the door and said that it was all very sad that old Mr Sweet Little (for Little was his family name, although we mostly ignored it) was about to kick the bucket. My parents were advised not to take my brother and me into the 'death room', seeing we were so young and all, but we were so much more accustomed to the death room than he that we ignored him and dashed in without giving his warning a second thought. I was almost in tears, for these deaths upset me fearfully, and the thought of how much depended on me and my brother (who was such a ham most of the time) made me very nervous.

The doctor was bending over the bed and turned back to tell us for at least the tenth time in the history of my family that, alas, old Mr Sweet Little was dying and that the children had best not see the face of implacable death. (I didn't know what 'implacable' was, but whatever it was, Mr Sweet was not!) My father pushed him rather abruptly out of the way saying, as he always did and very loudly for he was saying it to Mr Sweet, 'To hell with dying, man, these children want Mr Sweet' – which was my cue to throw myself upon the bed and kiss Mr Sweet all around the whiskers and under the eyes and around the collar of his nightshirt where he smelled so strongly of all sorts of things, mostly liniment.

I was very good at bringing him around, for as soon as I saw that he was struggling to open his eyes I knew he was going to be all right, and so could finish my revival sure of success. As soon as his eyes were open he would begin to smile and that way I knew that I had surely won. Once, though, I got a tremendous scare, for he could not open his eyes and later I learned that he had had a stroke and that one side of his face was stiff and hard to get into motion. When he began to smile I could tickle him in earnest because I was sure that nothing would get in the way of his laughter, although once he began to cough so hard that he almost threw me off his stomach, but that was when I was very small, little more than a baby, and my bushy hair had gotten in his nose.

When we were sure he would listen to us we would ask him why he was in bed and when he was coming to see us again and could we play with his guitar, which more than likely would be leaning against the bed. His eyes would get all misty and he would sometimes cry out loud, but we never let it embarrass us, for he knew that we loved him and that we sometimes cried too for no reason. My parents would leave the room to just the three of us; Mr Sweet, by that time, would be propped up in bed with a number of pillows behind his head and with me sitting and lying on his shoulder and along his chest. Even when he had trouble breathing he would not ask me to get down. Looking into my eyes he would shake his white head and run a scratchy old finger all around my hairline, which was rather low down, nearly to my eyebrows, and made some people say I looked like a baby monkey.

My brother was very generous in all this, he let me do all the revivaling – he had done it for years before I was born and so was glad to be able to pass it on to someone new. What he would do while I talked to Mr Sweet was pretend to play the guitar, in fact pretend that he was a young version of Mr Sweet, and it always made Mr Sweet glad to think that someone wanted to be like him – of course, we did not know this then, we played the thing by ear, and whatever he seemed to like, we did. We were desperately afraid that he was just going to take off one day and leave us.

It did not occur to us that we were doing anything special; we had not learned that death was final when it did come. We thought nothing of triumphing over it so many times, and in fact became a trifle contemptuous of people who let themselves be carried away. It did not occur to us that if our own father had been dying we could not have stopped it, that Mr Sweet was the only person over whom we had power.

When Mr Sweet was in his eighties I was studying in the university many miles from home. I saw him whenever I went home, but he was never on the verge of dying that I could tell and I began to feel that my anxiety for his health and psychological well-being was unnecessary. By this time he not only had a moustache but a long flowing snow-white beard, which I loved and combed and braided for hours. He was very peaceful, fragile, gentle, and the only jarring note about him was his old steel guitar, which he still played in the old sad, sweet, down-home blues way.

On Mr Sweet's ninetieth birthday I was finishing my doctorate in Massachusetts and had been making arrangements to go home for several weeks' rest. That morning I got a telegram telling me that Mr Sweet was dying again and could I please drop everything and come home. Of course I could. My dissertation could wait and my teachers would understand when I explained to them when I got back. I ran to the phone, called the airport, and within four hours I was speeding along the dusty road to Mr Sweet's.

The house was more dilapidated than when I was last there, barely a shack, but it was overgrown with yellow roses which my family had planted many years ago. The air was heavy and sweet and very peaceful. I felt strange walking through the gate and up the old rickety steps. But the strangeness left me as I caught sight of the long white beard I loved so well flowing down the thin body over the familiar quilt coverlet. Mr Sweet!

His eyes were closed tight and his hands, crossed over his stomach, were thin and delicate, no longer scratchy. I remembered how always before I had run and jumped up on him just anywhere; now I knew he would not be able to support my weight. I looked around at my parents, and was surprised to see that my father and mother also looked old and frail. My father, his own hair very gray, leaned over the quietly sleeping old man, who, incidentally, smelled still of wine and tobacco, and said, as he'd done so many times, 'To hell with dying, man! My daughter is home to see Mr Sweet!' My brother

had not been able to come as he was in the war in Asia. I bent down and gently stroked the closed eyes and gradually they began to open. The closed, wine-stained lips twitched a little, then parted in a warm, slightly embarrassed smile. Mr Sweet could see me and he recognised me and his eyes looked very spry and twinkly for a moment. I put my head down on the pillow next to his and we just looked at each other for a long time. Then he began to trace my peculiar hairline with a thin, smooth finger. I closed my eyes when his finger halted above my ear (he used to rejoice at the dirt in my ears when I was little), his hand stayed cupped around my cheek. When I opened my eyes, sure that I had reached him in time, his were closed.

Even at twenty-four how could I believe that I had failed, that Mr Sweet was really gone? He had never gone before. But when I looked up at my parents I saw that they were holding back tears. They had loved him dearly. He was like a piece of rare and delicate china which was always being saved from breaking and which finally fell. I looked long at the old face, the wrinkled forehead, the red lips, the hands that still reached out to me. Soon I felt my father pushing something cool into my hands. It was Mr Sweet's guitar. He had asked them months before to give it to me; he had known that even if I came next time he would not be able to respond in the old way. He did not want me to feel that my trip had been for nothing.

The old guitar! I plucked the strings, hummed 'Sweet Georgia Brown'. The magic of Mr Sweet lingered still in the cool steel box. Through the window I could catch the fragrant delicate scent of tender yellow roses. The man on the high old-fashioned bed with the quilt coverlet and the flowing white beard had been my first love.

Alice Walker

Activities

Title page

Discussion

1   What does the theme of 'Generations' mean to you?
2   Look at the photographs on page 147. Which of them best sum(s) up the theme and why?

Research and writing

Try to collect pictures of your own family based on this theme. Use it to help you write about *Old and young* in our family.

Partly because

Thinking about the poem

1   Explain in your words:
    what the mother wanted to tell her son,
    why she wanted to.
2   The second verse uses an image: a picture of the boy chasing butterflies. The mother thinks about what he might do to the butterflies when she is not there. What has this got to do with the first verse of the poem?
3   Would **you** rather be 'a kind seller of seeds' than 'an unkind lawyer'. What are your reasons?

Saturday song

As in any story, this one has many gaps. We have to fill in the gaps by using our imaginations and the clues that the writer has given us in the story. Try to work out what happened in the gaps in the story, especially, what happens to Peter at home and at school.

1   Go through the story carefully. Make a timetable of what actually happens at each stage.
2   Now make a list of any clues you have about what happens in between.
3   Use the clues and your own ideas to tell the story of what happens to Peter **between** his visits to Mr Briggs. Write it as a diary or as a short story.

The animal house

Writing a poem

Write about one of the following:

> your family
> your English group
> your friends
> any other group of people you know well

Write about them as:

> animals
> birds
> fish
> insects
> machines

The signature

Discussion

Think about your own memories of learning to read and write English.

1   Can you remember how you were taught?
2   What were the first books you remember reading?
3   Have you any particularly happy or unhappy memories of learning to read and write?

Writing

Imagine that the narrator shows the brown piece of paper with his mother's signature on it to a friend in the country where he now lives. They talk about it and he explains why he still carries it in his wallet. Write their conversation.

To hell with dying

Working on the story

Although the story concentrates on Mr Sweet, there are many clues in it about the life of the narrator. Work out as much as you can about these topics:

a)   what her home and family were like;
b)   what their neighbourhood was like;
c)   what she herself was like as a girl;
d)   what she did when she was a young woman.

Writing

Now write 'My impressions of the narrator in *To hell with dying* by Alice Walker.'

My life, my story

An aboriginal childhood

What kind of school?

I was left-handed. This was something that just didn't seem to matter one way or the other . . . until I went to school. Then I soon realised that the education department in those days considered it wrong for a child to write or sew with the left hand. There were many painful scenes when I refused to pick up a pencil with my right hand; many times the Head Teacher's ruler came down in full force on the knuckles of my left hand. I had to give in and write as best I could with my right hand. But for a long time I managed to hide from the sewing teacher the fact that I used my left hand for needlework.

When the sewing teacher picked up my piece of needlework to start off the sewing, she would begin with the needle and thread held in her right hand, sewing from right to left. Then she would hand the sample to me to continue the work, believing that I would sew in the same way. It didn't take me long to discover that by simply turning the work around, I could sew from left to right with my left hand.

I was always very careful to make sure no one saw what I was doing. I used to keep my head down and hold the piece of work below the desk while I sewed. I was good at needlework, and the teacher knew I could always be relied upon to turn in a good sample. She used to praise my work.

All went well until one morning when I sat as usual in the needlework class with my head bent over my sample. I longed to be outside in the hot sunshine. I heard the March flies buzzing against the window-panes, trapped like me inside the schoolroom. They would fly in on the wind, and were never able to get out again. My mind recalled the time when I once went to the window and tried to open it to free the flies, but the Head Teacher ordered me back to my seat and demanded to know why I had got up without permission. I couldn't explain. None of the white teachers would have understood. I just stared back at him, and he told me I was sullen and stubborn.

As my hands guided the needle from left to right, I dreamed about the world outside. I could hear the screeching of the blue mountain parrots calling and calling, trying to entice me out there...I thought of my little dinghy and my fishing-line, and the places where I could dig the fat sand worms that the large whiting could not resist as they came swimming on the incoming tide. I thought, another twenty minutes and I shall be free to run the mile home. By then, the tide will be just right for catching the big whiting.

I did not notice that the sewing teacher had left her table and was standing by me. Suddenly, two white hands were placed firmly on my desk. My mind was wrenched from dreams of fishing. I fixed my startled gaze on the small watch on the teacher's wrist.

'Look at me,' the teacher demanded.

I raised my eyes, then quickly dropped my gaze.

'You know you are forbidden to sew with your left hand!' the teacher told me in a loud, angry voice. 'How long have you been cheating me like this? You are a very stubborn, naughty girl!'

I could feel the eyes of all the other children turned full upon me. The teacher went on scolding me; she made me feel ashamed, then embarrassed – and at last very angry. I set my jaw, dropped my needlework sample on the floor, and brought my balled fists onto the desk.

'Don't you dare clench your fists like that,' the teacher said.

But I no longer cared what she said. I looked at my left hand, tightly clenched. It was always getting me into trouble. Suddenly I raised my left fist and smashed it down on the shiny face of the teacher's watch. I felt the wetness of blood. There was blood on the teacher's hand. Was it all my blood, I wondered.

The teacher gave a cry of pain and quickly withdrew her hands. She turned and fled from the classroom.

Presently, the Head Teacher came in. I had to walk the length of the shocked schoolroom. I stood silently before him as he flicked his cane. He caned me six times on each hand. I thought, my father will get a letter. It will demand payment for the broken wrist-watch. Yes, they will make him pay for the damage I have done.

Old Mac, the Head Teacher, was correcting a pile of exercise books. Sitting below his desk in the schoolroom, I watched as his pen crossed the paper. I tried to see whether it was my book he was busy with. When at last the books were given out, I opened mine and saw these words written in bold red ink across my homework: *Very bad, careless writing. Repeat exercise!*

I sighed, but I was not surprised. I was a very bad writer. My sisters and brothers were all good at writing, but I often had to repeat my exercises. My writing had been much better, before the teacher stopped me using my left hand.

That night, as I sat at the table at home with my two sisters, busy with homework, I looked at the hateful red writing in my exercise book and began to do last night's exercise all over again.

My elder sister had finished her homework and was peeling a banana. I envied her; she never seemed to have any trouble with schoolwork. She looked down at my book.

'Got another repeat?' she asked.

'I always get repeats,' I growled. 'You wouldn't like to do it for me, would you?'

She took a bite of banana. 'What's it worth?'

'I'll give you a penny.'

My sister pulled a face. 'Not enough.'

'Twopence?'

She shook her head.

'Threepence.'

She took another bite of banana, and smirked.

'All right. You know I've only got sixpence to my name. You can have it if you can disguise your handwriting to look like mine, only a bit neater.'

My sister thought for a while, then picked up the exercise book and studied my bad writing. 'Where's the money?' she asked.

'Can you really disguise your writing so that old schoolie Mac won't know it's yours?' I asked anxiously.

'Easy,' my sister answered confidently.

Soon she had finished writing out the exercise, and as she handed back the book she pocketed my sixpence.

Next day, when old Mac saw the rewritten exercise in my book, he looked long and hard at the writing, then called me out of the class.

'This is not your writing,' he told me sternly. 'Who wrote out the exercise for you?'

I refused to answer. I looked at the floor and remained silent. Then he called my elder sister to his table.

'Did you write out this exercise for your sister?' he asked, pointing to the book.

She saw no point in denying it, and admitted that she had done it. We were both caned for our deceit, and old Mac wrote right across the page in my exercise book in his bright-red ink: *Done by someone other than the owner of this book. Repeat!*

I returned to my desk filled with the humiliation of being found out. I had lost not only my precious sixpence, but also my right to be trusted. That red writing seemed to burn a hole in my mind. Yet what could I possibly do about my bad exercises? If I wrote them myself I always got repeats, and if I paid someone else to do them I got into trouble – and I still had to repeat them. I was really ashamed of the red writing in my book. It worried me far more than old Mac could ever imagine. I did try to write neatly, but somehow I just found it impossible. If only he would let me use my left hand instead of my right, I was sure I could turn in a neat exercise.

I did not like to think what my father would say if he found out how we had tried to cheat over my repeat exercise. That night, as I sat down to my homework, I hid the new red writing with my forearm as I began to copy out the exercise on the opposite page; I came to the conclusion that the only thing to do was to finish up that book as quickly as possible and throw it away before he had a chance to look at it. There would be plenty of sentences written in red ink in the next book – that was sure – but not the dreadful words that proclaimed our deceit.

I picked up my pen and wrote out the exercise again, and this time I did not make any pains over it at all. I knew perfectly well that my plan would mean I had to do more and more homework, but the sooner I filled the book, the better. Anyway, maybe if I went on scribbling and not caring, old Mac would get tired of putting 'Repeat!' on every page.

My sister looked over my shoulder and gasped. 'That's terrible writing! You'll get a repeat for sure.'

I didn't answer, but I thought fiercely: 'I hope I do. I sure hope I do.'

And my sister, looking sympathetic, quietly left me alone at the table.

Kath Walker

Early life of a steeplejack

A When I was a little lad I went to school like all little lads do. In those days the main road from Bolton to Manchester was made of blue cobbled stones and had two tram tracks down middle. I never liked going to school so me mother used to shove me on a tram, which then went rattling along the road. For the next mile and a half there were five chimney stacks to be counted and where I got off stood a great mass of them belching black smoke.

Every so often ladders painted bright red with men going up and down them appeared on the chimneys. When you are seven years old a man at the top of a 200ft high stack looks like someone from outer space. Those fellows really fascinated me, though the only two facts I knew about them were that they had red ladders and wore flat caps.

Then one morning after prayers, our headmaster announced he had a special treat for us kids. We were going to watch one of them great chimneys fall. In strict single file we were marched to a field at the back of the school and told to sit perfectly still. I remember we sat all morning, full of tension, waiting for that chimney to topple. It were still standing when we went home to midday dinner. On our return the stack lay on the ground and we had missed everything. . .

'I never saw it come down,' I told my parents. 'I never did.'

My school days rolled on and I kept seeing more red ladders on the chimneys around me. I never knew who owned them until years later. By then me father had an allotment beside a greyhound track on a site which had once been occupied by an old colliery. The chimney was standing and the chap who owned the site, which also had dog kennels and a café, decided it were time to get rid of the stack.

He engaged the services of some sort of mountain men from a place called Bacup. These characters arrived with ladders that had once been red but were now very wishy-washy. Anyway the men began by knocking off the top of the chimney. After that they chopped a big hole in the bottom and put in blocks of wood. I did not know what was going on though that were no matter. You see I had a ringside seat being allowed in the allotment with me father.

It were a right gloomy Sunday during winter and when the mountain men lit their fire under chimney the flames danced in the dark. The site owner also put on all the lights round his greyhound tracks which made us very excited. Then things began to go wrong. This was because not many chimneys were knocked down in those days and no one really knew what they were doing. The chimney came down sure enough, but it did not go right. I vividly recall the stack cutting the dog kennels in half and chopping a corner off the café. In addition it ripped down every power cable and all the lights went out. There were utter panic.

My next craze was to get a bike because everyone else seemed to have one. Even though me father slaved in a bleach factory and me mother at the gas works we never had any real money. Therefore a bike was something to be made by visiting tips. If you were lucky there would be a frame here and a couple of wheels somewhere else. After that came a pair of handlebars and you did not worry too much about brakes in them days.

The point was my bike enabled me to get about a bit searching for more things. By a fantastic stroke of luck I found an old pair of binoculars. I would then travel to and climb on top of the Earl of Bradford's slag heap. From there on clear summer nights I could survey the edges of Bolton and especially all them chimney stacks. It had to be summer for in winter you could not see for heavy smoke.

One clear summer night I spotted some strange black lines across the top of a chimney. They belonged to somebody's staging and next night I cycled right across town to have a closer look at what were going on. As I got nearer I saw red ladders with the name 'John Faulkner, Manchester' on their sides. Well you know how some fellows follow pop groups or football teams. From that evening my hero was John Faulkner.

I followed John Faulkner and his men who climbed chimneys around Bolton and Manchester. To my mind they did things right compared to others. Their staging when it appeared on top of a stack was square, symmetrical and solid looking with ropes coiled up all nice and neat. The others had crooked and funny looking staging with bits of rope blowing in the wind.

This were when I was still at school though not doing very well. I was no good at reading and writing so they put the likes of me in the art group. There we painted vases of flowers and bowls of apples. Also when our teacher felt like it we would go for walks with our drawing books. Of course you could not go anywhere without seeing chimneys. Not only did I draw all the chimneys but I put in red ladders and staging.

'What have you put those in for?' my teacher would ask and I answered, 'It were in my mind.'

B *When he was a little older, Fred Dibnah took to doing daring stunts. He used to find places where steeplejacks had put ladders up and climb to the top of the building for fun.*

We then came up with the idea of a dummy to look like a man hanging from the top of another chimney. Mr Rawlinson* always went home for his dinner, so I started constructing the fake corpse out of wood lathes and fencing wire. It were basically one straight stick for the backbone and a stick the other way for the arms. Coiled wire made the torso, then there were a bit of board for the pelvis with legs dangling downwards. I made the head from a sackful of old rags.

Next we had to dress this dummy, which called for all our ingenuity. My mate's wife were always going to jumble sales and she had got a monstrous overcoat which he did not like. I supplied some old pants and a pair of me father's boots filled with concrete to make the hanging look right. The body folded over at the shoulders so I could tie the whole thing in the form of a haversack.

The stack I selected was 212ft tall and situated on a road near the town centre. John Faulkner's men were working on this chimney with their red ladders all in position. Although we went there by night, all the factory lights were on and the boilers going full blast. Me mate took me as near as possible to the place, but it still meant negotiating about 24 back gardens before getting to where I wanted.

The climb were no trouble. Soon them lights were twinkling away far below me before they sort of faded. It were pitch black when I reached the staging and as I started to untie the dummy, the wind got inside it. How it ended up was quite unbelievable. Its legs were still over the shoulders while the rope for hanging it came under the crutch. Worse still the whole thing spun like a propeller.

* *Fred's boss*

I thought, 'This isn't going to be a success' and tried to drag it back again, fighting against the wind at 212ft. But it were no good. The dummy was being blown outwards at 45° and for a man supposed to be hanging himself it looked horrible. So I just came down that chimney, bought myself some fish and chips and went home.

The next day was a foggy Saturday with no wind. As bad luck would have it, I were working on the other side of town. I could hardly wait for 12 o'clock. The moment it was knocking off time I set off for the chimney, sort of like the crow flies. I went through gardens, across a cemetery and along the Bolton to Blackpool railway line.

When I reached the chimney area there was no sign of the hanging dummy, but groups of people stood at street corners as though there had been some sort of disaster. I said to a couple of women and a fellow,

'What's going on like?'

'Some silly sod,' this fellow replied, 'hung a dummy from the top of that chimney.'

'Go away,' I said. 'What happened?'

Then the women started telling me – together. It seems that an old boy who lived on the main road across the mill woke up at first light, looked out of the window and saw the dreadful spectacle. Soon the whole neighbourhood was up and about with one person after another ringing up the police, the fire brigade and ambulances.

'The mill manager was dragged out of bed,' one of the women kept saying in a knowing way. 'Dragged out of bed.'

'Then they dragged John Faulkner's foreman out of bed,' said the other. 'They knocked him up then got him down here. The police told him he would have to climb the chimney and retrieve the dead body.'

Shortly afterwards, I learned, someone arrived with a pair of binoculars and those in the know realised it were a practical joke. Nevertheless John Faulkner's foreman had to bring down the dummy for analysis like. In the pocket of the jumble sale overcoat they found a Manchester bus ticket and the university students again got the blame.

The story did not quite end there. Some time later Mr Rawlinson had me fitting a new floor in a semi near to the self-same chimney. The lady of the house was very talkative, so I asked her weren't that the stack from which the Manchester students hung a dummy? To my amazement, she broke into a hell of a frenzy.

'It may have been a dummy,' she said all fierce like, 'but my husband didn't know that and had a heart attack.'

'A heart attack,' I gulped.

'Fortunately he got over it,' she continued to my relief, 'but it were a bad sort of thing.'

Fred Dibnah

The choosing

We were first equal Mary and I
with the same coloured ribbons in mouse-coloured hair,
and with equal shyness
we curtseyed to the lady councillor
for copies of Collins' Children's Classics.
First equal, equally proud.

Best friends too Mary and I
a common bond in being cleverest (equal)
in our small school's small class.
I remember
the competition for top desk
or to read aloud the lesson
at school service.
And my terrible fear
of her superiority at sums.

I remember the housing scheme
Where we both stayed.
The same house, different homes,
where the choices were made.

I don't know exactly why they moved,
but anyway they went.
Something about a three-apartment
and a cheaper rent.
But from the top deck of the high-school bus
I'd glimpse among the others on the corner
Mary's father, mufflered, contrasting strangely
with the elegant greyhounds by his side.

He didn't believe in high-school education,
especially for girls,
or in forking out for uniforms.

Ten years later on a Saturday –
I am coming home from the library –
sitting near me on the bus,
Mary
with a husband who is tall,
curly haired, has eyes
for no one else but Mary.
Her arms are round the full-shaped vase
that is her body.
Oh, you can see where the attraction lies
in Mary's life –
not that I envy her, really.

And I am coming from the library
with my arms full of books.
I think of the prizes that were ours for the taking
and wonder when the choices got made
we don't remember making.

Liz Lochhead

Dear Diary

Judy Blume is a well-known novelist. She receives thousands of letters from children and teenagers about their lives and their problems. In this extract from her book Dear Judy she writes about keeping – and reading – diaries.

Dear Judy,
    From now on you're going to be getting a lot of letters from me. I'm going to tell you everything that's on my mind. Things that I can't tell my parents or my friends. You don't have to answer every letter. I know you've got other things to do. I just like writing to you. It's like talking to a friend.

Kelly, age 13

    So many kids write to me because the act of writing down what's on their minds is often enough to help them feel better. That's why, when I write back to them, I suggest that they get a notebook or a diary or journal – it doesn't really matter – and write in it whenever they feel the need. Journal writing might not be for everyone, but for kids who feel comfortable with the idea, and for kids who write easily, it can be a valuable tool – one that lasts a lifetime.

Dear Judy,
    Last Christmas a friend gave me a diary. Although I had started to keep diaries before I never really committed myself to them. This diary, though, saved my sanity and perhaps, my life. This diary made me want to write. It helped me through the most difficult year of my life. It lifted me out of a gloominess that nearly ended in suicide. It took away the hurt, added to my few joys, relieved my anger and halted my tears.
    As I read back through my diary one statement I see at the bottom of an October page sort of explains what I felt this year. *I'm scared . . . I'm so scared. I wish somebody would talk to me and tell me it's going to be all right.*
    This whole year everything I went through I went through all *alone.* I've promised myself that from now on I will find someone to talk to. But a promise to yourself is too easy to break so I am promising you and this will make me think twice before going back on my word.
    This is a year I will never forget. I have grown and learned in many ways.

Missy, age 14

I was given a five-year diary when I was in fifth grade. It had a brown leather cover and a tiny lock and key. The dates were printed on each page in gold ink. I thought it was beautiful and I loved the idea of writing in it every day. But I didn't know what I was supposed to write and so, I hardly wrote in it at all. Soon I became discouraged and gave up. I wasn't ready for a diary.

Janice, a mother who wrote to me last year, said that she had given a diary to her daughter, Christine, for her tenth birthday. A week later, when Janice went to Christine's room to kiss her goodnight, she found Christine in tears. 'What's wrong?' Janice asked. 'I can't think of anything to write in my diary!' Christine sobbed, throwing it across the room. Janice blamed herself for choosing a gift that made Christine feel like a failure. Christine wasn't ready for a diary either.

If you do give your kids a diary tell them that they don't have to write in it every day. That's the whole point. There are no rules. Encourage your kids to write whenever they feel like it and assure them that you will respect their privacy.

I began to keep a diary again when I was in high school. I found it satisfying to confide in my diary, as many teenagers do. But to protect myself, in case – God forbid – my mother ever found it, I invented code words so that she would not know what I was talking about.

Dear Judy,
I have a story to tell you. It is about a black girl who had no one to talk to. She did have a lot of friends but no one that she could really sit down and talk to. Not even her own mother would talk to her, for her mother was far too busy to have a few words with her oldest daugher. She was the oldest of five children. She had a stepfather but he was never home. They all lived in a small apartment.

Because she had no one to talk to she kept everything to herself. She was very smart but she had a lot on her mind. She would daydream and sometimes act dumb. That was not good. She even got sick a lot!

Someone noticed what was going on and saw that she was an intelligent girl with too much on her mind. So a diary was given to her for Christmas and she liked the idea of having one. It helped her unload a lot that was on her mind. It became the one true friend she had.

But her mother never liked the idea of her having the diary. So months later her mother started to read it and found out a lot of things about her that she didn't like. The girl found out and tried to run away but she had nowhere to go so she went back home. Her mother found out why she ran away and took the diary away. Her mother even tried to use the diary and what the girl had written in it against her.

Now the girl hates everyone and everything. The story goes on to tell what the girl goes through with her family and how she may go crazy.

Francesca, age 16

Toward the end of my seventeenth summer I discovered that my mother had been reading my diary. I knew because, to ensure my privacy, I had devised an intricate way of wrapping rubber bands around it and one day I noticed that they had not been properly replaced.

It was the summer of 1955 and my parents and I were driving from New Jersey to California, to visit relatives. I was bored on the long, hot, dusty drive and wished I had taken a job at a summer camp instead. I missed my friends and I longed for excitement. I was moody, sullen and irritable. I wrote about my hostile feelings in my diary every night.

I was furious at my mother when I found out she had read my diary. (And I was also embarrassed by what I had written. The code words I'd invented covered my love life, which was nonexistent that summer, but not my feelings about travelling with my family.) Still, I didn't confront my mother right away. Instead, I slept with my diary under my pillow every night and didn't let it out of my sight during the day. Months later, when I finally did confront my mother, she confessed that she had read my diary that summer because I had seemed so unhappy. She thought it might give her a clue as to what was wrong. I could not forgive her for reading my diary and I vowed that when I had children I would respect their privacy.

But when Randy (*Judy Blume's daughter*) was sixteen she seemed to change, almost overnight. I felt as if I didn't know her anymore. One day, when she didn't return from school as expected, and I was worried sick, I went to her room. I found her diary on a shelf in the closet. I sat on her bed for a long time, holding the diary, blaming myself for everything that had gone wrong. In spite of my vow to respect her privacy, I finally opened it and read the last few entries. It was clear that she was feeling alienated, frightened and confused and that we needed help.

When she finally returned, late that night, I told her I had read some of her diary. I still don't know if she was more angry or more relieved. With help we began to work out our problems.

I can't excuse myself for having read Randy's diary. I don't want my kids or anyone else to read my journal. What I write tonight may have nothing to do with how I am feeling tomorrow. I tend to write in my journal when I am troubled, confused, tense or angry. I find that writing about whatever is on my mind relieves the tension and helps me sort out my feelings. Often it is just the mood of the moment. I rarely write about my good times. I'm not interested in keeping a record of my life. Writing in my journal offers me an emotional outlet.

Judy Blume

Working late

A light is on in my father's study
'Still up?' he says, and we are silent,
looking at the harbor lights,
listening to the surf
and the creak of coconut boughs.

He is working late on cases.
No impassioned speech! He argues from evidence,
actually pacing out and measuring,
while the fans revolving on the ceiling
winnow the true from the false.

Once he passed a brass curtain rod
through a head made out of plaster
and showed the jury the angle of fire –
where the murderer must have stood.
For years, all through my childhood,
if I opened a closet . . . bang!
There would be the dead man's head
with a black hole in the forehead.

All the arguing in the world
will not stay the moon.
She has come all the way from Russia
to gaze for a while in a mango tree
and light the wall of a veranda,
before resuming her interrupted journey
beyond the harbor and the lighthouse
at Port Royal, turning away
from land to the open sea.

Yet, nothing in nature changes, from that day to this,
she is still the mother of us all.
I can see the drifting offshore lights,
black posts where the pelicans brood.

And the light that used to shine
at night in my father's study
now shines as late in mine.

Louis Simpson

Third person narratives

These pieces of writing were done by pupils of Nailsea School, Avon, as part of their work on autobiography.

A

The long summer evening was just beginning as the eleven-year-old made her way home from her friend's house where she had been for the afternoon and tea. As the sun dropped behind the row of tall trees – they were tall to her – she felt the welcoming coolness of a summer's evening and sighed. Turning into the driveway to the house the girl made her way past the familiar old company car which was badly in need of attention; the rust eroded the paintwork in patches across the chassis and the weight of the carpentry tools in the back heavily tested the suspension.

Once inside Gill announced her return to her parents, who automatically replied either by voice or by glance. The television chattered noisily in the corner of the room; this was the usual means of entertainment every evening – it could be tedious at times.

It was 7.30 pm. Recounting the events of the day and reliving the interview at the Comprehensive School was the first task of the girl as she sat next to her mother on the settee. Her father paid no attention whatsoever, being content to watch the show on the screen in front of him and eating his supper. Gill resented his lack of involvement; she realised his interest in what she did was minimal, but nevertheless, she felt hurt.

It was 7.45 pm. Abruptly her father rose, mumbling an explanation and leaving the room. Her mother, startled at this sudden departure, followed him quickly. The eleven year old sat, unconcerned.

It was 8.00 pm. The phone-bell cried out once and then was dead – her mother had rung someone. Moving quietly to the bottom of the stairs she watched the worried face of her mother peer downwards before descending.

"Your father's not well, love. I've just rung the doctor, she'll be here in a minute.'

Her stomach churned.

It was twenty minutes before the doctor arrived and another ten before Gill was told what was happening. She broke it to her gently, just before the ambulance arrived.

As she said these few words she was calm and positive, her face one of controlled, hidden fear.

'They're taking him to the hospital. He's going to be OK.'

Turning her back on the confused child, she turned to her husband's side. The dying sun filtered through the windows, the light of its rays blinding the screen of the television which still droned, oblivious to the real anguish which filled the atmosphere in the house. The child stood before it, unable to see.

B

She couldn't remember why it was that it had to be this way, but it didn't really matter. There was a dark and aimless feeling about the whole situation. She couldn't understand for the life of her what, or even why, it was happening to her. It was just so sudden.

What would he think when he returned to an empty flat, all the furniture moved out just as it had been before they arrived? It was almost a year since then. During the time they had lived there they must have walked out about six times. But this time they would not be going back.

Her mother placed a cheque on top of the fireplace. She asked her mother why the cheque? She didn't understand that her mother owed him money. Her mother had replied that it made her feel better. They were always shouting at each other and often he used to make out that her mother owed him a lot. Not just the money, but everything.

She could not believe this, maybe because this was her mother, or maybe because she could not remember her mother ever upsetting him the way he upset her. But, all the same, she felt bad, as if she had betrayed him, which now, looking back on it, seemed a stupid emotion to feel. After all, what had he ever done for her? Oh, he was nice to her all right, but he never gave her the impression that he was at all interested in her.

She didn't mind this, she could live with it; through a lot of her life she had not had a father-figure so she could quite easily live without one. It was her mother she was worried about. She was taking it all very well now, but what about a couple of months from now? How would she cope then?

Her mother put her coat on and very boldly walked out. She followed, looking back as she left. Her mother drove the car. She went in the removal van with the removal men. It was exciting. She was right up high in the front of a lorry. She probably would never have a ride in one again.

She stopped feeling bad, and thought to herself, maybe, just maybe, everything would be all right now . . .

C

A few friends called her over. She knew what they wanted as she fixed her eyes on the familiar wall her friends were stood by. As she walked quickly towards them, she smiled at a group of boys playing marbles on the grate.

When she reached the wall her friends had started without her. Handstands. A fun girls' activity. Often girls practised handstands against the wall. But today it was going to be different.

At her first try she didn't quite make the wall. Then tucking her skirt up again, she tried again. Then another, then another. Then her friends cried, 'Do a crab, Crawl down the wall.' She was good at that and did so with a grin. Then she tried it again but was too close to the wall and got stuck. A group of boys jeered at her and, collapsing to the floor, she yelled, 'Go away, creeps!'

The boys laughed. One of the taller boys came forward. The boys were a year younger than her and she felt humiliated and angry that she had to put up with them. The boy laughed again and then said, 'And here we have the champion handstander.' All the boys roared with laughter – not that she could find anything extremely funny about his statement.

'I'd like to see you try,' she shouted.

'We're boys!' the boy said and pushed past her. She turned and pushed him, to send him flying against the wall. Then it happened. He kicked out at her. She put her hand down to meet his foot to stop his foot from making contact with her body. Pain ran through her hand and up her arm. But pain wasn't enough to make her cry. She walked slowly away into the building and then looked down at her hand. A small, clenched hand with an extremely bent thumb. More bent than it should have been. Tears stung her eyes. She tried to move it, but nothing. Her thumb wouldn't budge. Then she screamed and tears ran down her face.

The old dinner lady waddled towards her.

'What's wrong dear?' came a soft gentle voice.

'He's broke it,' she yelled, 'He's broke my hand.' She screamed again. The dinner lady took her hand.

'I'm sure he hasn't. It just hurts a little.' Then she screamed over and over again.

'He's broke my hand, he's broke my hand.'

The strong smell of disinfectant reached her as she walked into the Infirmary, the arm of her favourite teacher around her shoulder, comforting her.

The hours of waiting. Her teacher gone, replaced by her mother. She was right, she thought, as she looked down at the large white plaster stretching from her thumb to her elbow. She was right, she thought again. He's broke my hand.

Activities

An aboriginal childhood

What kind of school?

As you read the two stories, you can build up a picture of the school that Kath Walker went to: the teachers, how they treated the children, what happened in the classroom.

1   Read both stories and make a note of all the information you can get about the school.
2   Use your notes as the basis for a piece of writing about the school.
3   Read what you have written: what do you think of the school and its teachers? Write a paragraph expressing your opinions.

Right-handed world

The way Kath Walker was treated used to be common in many countries, including Britain. Nowadays left-handed people are treated a little more considerately. But there are still problems.

1   Think about parts of everyday life where being left-handed is still a disadvantage. Make a list of them.
2   Make a list of any ways in which being left-handed can be an advantage.
3   Think about ways in which life could be made easier for people who are left-handed. (For example, are there inventions which would make mechanical tasks easier?)
4   Use the notes you have made as the basis for a piece of writing.

Early life of a steeplejack

Character

What impression do you get of Fred Dibnah from these extracts? Read them through again and make notes on his character:

    what he 'sounds like' as you read
    his interests and enthusiasms
    how he got on with people
    his sense of humour
    any other points that strike you

Now use these notes to help you write a description of his character.

The choosing

Writing

We see this story from one point of view: 'I'. How do you think Mary remembers the events the poem describes? Suppose that she did see the narrator on the bus and that this starts her, too, thinking about their schooldays and what followed. Think about all this and then tell *Mary's story*.

Dear Diary

Discussion

Talk about the letters and Judy Blume's comments.

1   What are the main points that she is making?
2   Do you agree with her or not? What are your reasons?
3   What do you think of her behaviour when she read the diary?
4   What would you have done, if you had been her?

Writing

There are a number of times in this extract when a daughter talks to her mother.

1   Choose one of them.
2   Imagine how the conversation might have gone. Think what **you** would have said if you had been a) the daughter, b) the mother.
3   Write the conversation as a script.

Working late

Questions to think about

1   This poem works through a series of pictures. Which of them were most vivid to you when you read it? For each one quote the words and describe the picture that those words produced in your mind.
2   Near the end of the poem the writer talks about 'that day and this'. What were the two days he is thinking about? And what has happened in between?
3   What is the point of the section of the poem (starting, 'All the arguing in the world...') that describes the moon?
4   How would you describe the general feeling of this poem and why?

Third person narratives

These pieces were written by school pupils aged 14–17. They were using the *Autobiography* unit on pages 53–64. In particular they were working on pages 60–62, on the idea of writing about yourself as if you were someone else. Read all the pieces. Choose the one you like best. Think about this piece and then write a commentary on it, saying what it is that you like about it and where you think it could be improved.

Acknowledgements

The publishers would like to thank the following for permission to reproduce photographs and other copyright material:

All Sport p.50; **Aspect Picture Library** p.134 (top); **Australia House** p.171; **Australian Information Service** p.174; **B.B.C. Enterprises Limited** p.120; **Linda Bartlett/Colorific** p.135 (2nd from bottom); **Anne Bolt** pp.86/87 (background), p.159; **Compix** p.91 (left); **Crown Copyright/Ordnance Survey Southampton** p.66; **Daily Telegraph** p.97 (top, bottom); **Fred Dibnah** p.175; **Format Photographers Ltd/Maggie Murray** pp.22 (bottom right), p.147 (bottom left); **Fortean Picture Library/ René Dahinden** pp.10 (all), p.14 (top, middle); **Frank Green** pp.75 (top left, top right, bottom); **Sally & Richard Greenhill** pp.134 (bottom), p.135 (2nd from top), p.147 (top right), p.187; **Jeremy Hartley/ OXFAM** p.85 (top left); **Jeremy Hartley/Voluntary Service Overseas** p.87 (inset); **Hunting Aerofilms** p.96 (top, bottom); **Hutchison Library** p.86 (top, bottom); **Impact Photos/Homes Sykes** p.135 (bottom); **Intermediate Technology** pp.90, 91 (right); **Photo Coop** p.186 (top left); **Photo Coop/Gina Glover** p.147; **Laurie Sparham/Network** p.188; **Split Second** p.51; **Syndication International** pp.22 (top right, bottom left), p.56 (top, middle, bottom); **Patty Tarbet/Eastman's Studio** p.14 (bottom); **The National Gallery** p.144; **Marcus Thompson/OXFAM** p.85 (bottom left); **Penny Tweedie/Save the Children Fund** p.85 (top right); **Voluntary Service Overseas** pp.89, 92 (top left, bottom right, right); Additional photography by Martin Chillmaid and Rob Judges.

The illustrations are by: Tracey Agate, Jenny Beck, Judy Brown, Jenny Bech, Lynne Chapman, Penny Dann, Rosamund Fowler, Mike Hingley, Richard Hook, Mark Hackett, David Mitcheson, Peter Melnyczuk, Mike Nicholson, Jenny Norton, Mark Oldroyd, Julia Quenzler, Nigel Paige, Chris Price, Malcolm Sparkes, Susan Scott, Nick Sharratt, Deryk Thomas, Stephen Wilkin, Kathryn Ward

The authors are grateful to the following Advisers for their help in the early stages of this project: Iain Ball, Philip Crumpton, Pat D'Arcy, Kevin Jeffery, Nick Jones, Gervase Phinn, Anne Thomas

The authors are grateful to the following for their comments on the project whilst in progress: Richard Bates, Roy Henderson, David Kitchen, Roger Knight, Mary McKinlay

The authors are grateful to the following teachers for their help in trialling material for this book: Mr Nicholls, Elliott Durham School, Nottingham   Mr Carver, St. Andrews School, Leatherhead   Mr Jarvis, Sir John Gleed Girls' School, Spalding   Mrs Charman, Castle Hills School, Gainsborough   Mrs Maule, Parklands School, Leeds   Mr Barret, St. John Fisher School, Dewsbury   Mr McMaster, Robert Napier School, Gillingham   Mr Jordan, William Penn School, Dulwich   Mr Phillips, Horsell School, Horsell   Mrs Henman, Beverley School, New Malden   Mr Jeffrey, Richard Challoner School, New Malden   Ms Hoather, St. John the Baptist School, Kingfield   Mr D'Arcy, Rising Brook School, Stafford   Mrs Chapman, Brookhouse School, Stoke-on-Trent   Mr Combes, Pindar School, Scarborough   Mr James, St. Laurence School, Bradford on Avon   Mr Eames, Wootton Bassett School, Wootton Bassett   Ms Tilling, Scalby School, Newby   Mr Walton, Ridgeway School, Swindon   Mr Gilchrist, Backwell School, Backwell   Ms Pratchett, Sir Bernard Lovell School, Bristol   Mr Webster, Chew Valley School, Bristol   Mr Robinson, Broadoak Secondary School, Weston-Super-Mare

We are grateful for permission to include the following copyright material:

James Berry: 'Girls can we educate we dads?'. By permission of the author.   **Judy Blume:** 'Dear Diary' from *Letters to Judy* (1986). Reprinted by permission of William Heinemann Limited.   **Ray Bradbury:** 'The Flying Machine' from *The Stories of Ray Bradbury* (Granada 1983). Reprinted by permission of Grafton Books, a division of the Collins Publishing Group.   **Sandy Brechin:** 'The Animal House'. Copyright the author.**   **Sid Chaplin:** 'The Shaft' from *The Leaping Lad* (Longman, 1971). Reprinted by permission of David Higham Associates Limited.   **Fred Dibnah:** 'Early Life of a Steeplejack' from *Fred Dibnah: Steeplejack* (Line One Studio Ltd.)**   **U.A. Fanthorpe:** 'Not My Best Side' from *Selected Poems* Reprinted by permission of Peterloo Poets.   **Zulfikar Ghose:** 'Geography Lesson' from *Jets from Orange* (Macmillan, London 1967). © Zulfikar Ghose 1967. Reprinted by permission of the author.   **Liliana Heker:** 'The Stolen Party' from *Other Fires* edited by A. Manguel, published by Picador. Reprinted by permission of Pan Books Limited.   **Clyde Hosein:** 'The Signature' from *The Killing of Nelson John* (London Magazine Editions 1980). Reprinted with permission.   **Shirley Jackson:** 'After you my dear Alphonse' from *Spectrum* II, edited by Bennett, Cowan, and Hay. (Longman 1970). Reprinted with permission.   **Ursula Laird:** 'Partly because'. Copyright the author.**   **Tom Leonard:** 'The qualification' from *Intimate Voices* (Galloping Dog Press). Reprinted by permission of the author.   **Liz Lochhead:** 'Men Talk' from *True Confessions and New Cliches*. and 'The Choosing' from *Dreaming Frankenstein and Collected Poems*. Reprinted by permission of Polygon Press.   **Maureen Monaghan:** 'Saturday Song'. Copyright the author**   **R.K. Narayan:** 'The Watchman' from *Under the Banyan Tree*. Reprinted by permission of William Heinemann Limited.   **Oodgeroo of the tribe Noonuccal** custodian of the land Minjerribah (formerly Kath Walker): 'The Left-hander' from *Stradbroke Dreamtime* by Oodgeroo Noonuccal. © Oodgeroo Noonuccal, 1972. Reprinted by permission of Angus & Robertson.   **Craig Raine:** 'A Martian Sends a Postcard Home' from *A Martian Sends a Postcard Home*. © Craig Raine 1979. Reprinted by permission of Oxford University Press.   **Len Rush:** 'The New Place' from *Northern Drift* compiled by A. Bradley. (Blackie & Son, 1980). Reprinted by permission of the author.   **Louis Simpson:** 'Working Late' from *Caviare at the Funeral*. © Louis Simpson 1981. Reprinted by permission of Oxford University Press.   **Henry Slesar:** script material adapted from *The Examination Room*. Copyright the author, c/o Campbell, Thompson and McLaughlin.**   **Kurt Vonnegut Jr.:** 'Harrison Bergeron' from *Welcome to the Monkey House* (1968). Reprinted by permission of Jonathan Cape Limited.   **Alice Walker:** 'To hell with dying' from *In Love and Trouble* (Women's Press, 1984). Reprinted by permission of David Higham Associates Limited.   **Robert Westall:** 'St George and the Dragons.' Printed with permission of the author.   'Third Person Narratives', all by pupils at The Nailsea School, Avon. Reprinted with permission.

Every effort has been made to contact copyright holders before publication, however in some cases ** this has not been possible. If contacted the publisher will ensure that full credit is given at the earliest opportunity.
Cover photo: Science Photo Library/Melvin Prueitt/Los Alamos Laboratory